ABOUT THE AUTHOR

Robert Langs, M.D., is Visiting Clinical Researcher, Nathan S. Kline Center for Psychiatric Research, Orangeburg, New York; Visiting Clinical Professor, Mt. Sinai School of Medicine, New York City; and Lecturer at the New School for Social Research, New York City. Dr. Langs is the author of more than thirty books on psychotherapy and psychoanalysis dealing with such topics as science, systems, communication, and interaction. He is in private practice in New York City.

UNCONSCIOUS COMMUNICATION IN EVERYDAY LIFE

UNCONSCIOUS COMMUNICATION IN EVERYDAY LIFE

ROBERT LANGS, M.D.

JASON ARONSON INC.
Northvale, New Jersey
London

Library of Congress Cataloging-in-Publication Data

Langs, Robert J.
  Unconscious communication in everyday life.

  Bibliography: p. 199
  Includes index.
  1. Interpersonal communication   2. Nonverbal commuunication (Psy-
chology) 3. Subconsciousness. I. Title.
BF637.C45L36   153.6   82-1669
ISBN 1-56821-106-6 (softcover)   AACR2

Manufactured in the United States of America. Jason Aronson Inc. offers books and cassettes. For information and catalog write to Jason Aronson Inc., 230 Livingston Street, Northvale, New Jersey 07647.

CONTENTS

Preface   xi

Part I   ENCODING AND DECODING MESSAGES

1. Two Forms of Expression   3
   A Psychological Paradox
   Encoding as Emotional Protection
   Some Historical Perspectives
   Analyzing Emotional Triggers
2. Perspectives on Human Communication   9
   Communication as Essential to Survival
   Two Parables of Communication
   The Human Child as Communicator
   Single and Multiple Messages
   The Ideal Mixture
3. Surface Messages   17
   Some Word Derivations
   A Message Versus a Communication
   The Message in Isolation
   The Role of Context
   Message Forms
   The Motives Behind Messages
   Inner- and Outer-Directed Messages
   The Presence of Meaning in Messages

True and False Messages
Validation

4. Thinking Outside of Awareness   31
   Two Types of Messages
   Unconscious Encoding
   Mechanisms of Primary Process
   The Mental World Outside of Our Awareness
   Hypnotism and Freudian Slips

5. Conscious Encoding   41
   Deliberate Encoding
   Conscious Vertical Encoding
   The Derivative Message
   Responding to Encoded Messages
   Representability
   The Use of Communication Versus Meaning
   Triggers and Context
   The Mechanisms of Conscious Encoding
   Encoding Mechanisms Work Together

6. Unconscious Encoding: An Introduction   55
   A Woman Is Sawed in Half
   A Magic Show
   Boy Kills Girl
   Girl Castrates Boy
   A Parent Dies

7. Unconscious Encoding: Origins with Freud   61
   Dream Work and Dream Thought
   Day Residue
   Freud's Self-Analysis

8. Unconscious Encoding in Our Daily Lives   69
   "You've Been Aloof All Night"
   The Dialogue's Unconscious Encoding: Isabel
   The Dialogue's Unconscious Encoding: John

9. Indications of the Presence of Unconscious   79
   Encoding
   Overdecoding and Underdecoding
   Indicators of Hidden Messages
   Seven Signs of Hidden Messages

10. Direct and Contextual (Trigger) Decoding   89
    Direct Decoding
    Contextual or Trigger Decoding

Two Triggers for One Scene
Validation in Social Settings
A Delicate Balance

Part II   HIDDEN MESSAGES IN OUR
            DAILY LIVES

11. The Direct Decoding of Dreams   111
    A Dreamer and His Dream
    Responding to the Surface of the Dream
12. The Trigger Decoding of Dreams   119
    Searching for Triggers
    Conscious Versus Unconscious Fantasies
13. Hidden Triggers and Their Consequences   129
    Bill's Analytic Hour

Part III   MEANING AND NONMEANING, TRUTH AND LIE

14. Styles of Communication   147
    The Truth Sender and Receiver
    The Lie Sender and Receiver
    Styles of Unconscious Communication
15. Truth Senders and Truth Receivers   153
    The Choice to Flee or Fight
    A Knight to the Rescue
    The Search for Truth
16. Lie Senders and Lie Receivers   161
    Pseudo-Insights
    Failure to Recognize Lies
    Nonderivative Lies
    Derivative Lies
    Lie Narration
    The Lie Sender
    Lie Systems in a Culture
    Sharing Lies
    Common Types of Unconscious Liars
    The Lie Receiver (Truth Obliterator)
17. Dumpers   177
    Quiet and Noisy Messages
    Truth Dumpers and Lie Dumpers
    Metabolism
    Dump Receivers Are Dump Senders

18. Role and Image Evocations   183
    An Illustration with Aspects of Dumping
19. Communicative Styles in Daily Interactions   187
    The Importance of Quiet Reflection
    Achieving Insight through Reflection
    Procedures for Self-Analysis
    Dumping as Inimical to Self-Analysis
    The Interplay of Communicative Styles
    The Communicative Style of This Book

References   199
Index   201

PREFACE

This book is a study of human communication, conscious and especially unconscious. At its heart are the rediscovery and elaboration of a specific method for decoding hidden messages, first described by Freud in 1900 in his masterpiece, *The Interpretation of Dreams*. This approach is called *trigger decoding* since a message is deciphered entirely in light of its stimulus—the experience that set it off. Founded on the basic thesis that human communication is both internally motivated (intrapsychically based) and interactionally determined (interpersonal), this type of decoding eliminates the arbitrary qualities so characteristic of the usual efforts we make in trying to identify the presence of hidden messages in a variety of human expressions. The result is a decoding method that provides access to emotionally critical encoded expressions, and which is relatively simple, highly specific, immediately dynamic, and alive with cogent meaning.

The book begins by giving attention to the surface of messages, and it moves quickly into mental functioning and communication as they take place outside of the direct awareness of senders and/or receivers. The methods we use, both consciously and unconsciously, to *encode* disturbing *raw messages* are clarified and illustrated. The use of trigger *decoding* and its many ramifications are then discussed in detail.

The application of trigger decoding to a wide range of messages from a variety of message senders reveals two basic styles of unconscious communication: *truth senders* and *receivers*, and *lie* or *lie-barrier senders* and *receivers*. The first group meaningfully represents and encodes the conscious and unconscious, manifest and latent, meanings and implications of a painful emotional situation—a traumatic trigger. In contrast, the second group destroys such meaning and with it meaningful relatedness; in place of the truth, lie senders and receivers express lies or fictions while also erecting powerful barriers against truthful realizations. This fundamental classification is the key to understanding many problems in human communication.

The book is designed for the practical goal of helping the reader to learn how to decode the hidden messages in his or her own communicative expressions, as well as those from others. It offers a means by which communicative styles can be identified and, where necessary, constructively modified. It brings a dimension of insight into our daily lives that should enhance our understanding of ourselves and those to whom we relate.

This volume is a consequence of some ten years of psychoanalytic investigation into the nature of the therapeutic interaction and experience (Langs 1978, 1979, 1980, 1981, 1982a, 1982b). These studies were founded on the discovery of the critical role played by the triggers for communications from patients. The realization that these stimuli for emotional response in individuals engaged in psychotherapy virtually always involve the interventions of the therapist led to major revisions in the understanding of the therapeutic situation. It is the intention of the present volume to carry these insights over into the communicative experiences of all persons in their daily lives.

The present book is intended as a statement of emotionally meaningful truths. Because of our natural attraction to defenses and lie-barrier formations, we all have a noticeable tendency to create and seek out clichéd and therefore essentially meaningless and false solutions to our emotional problems and distress. The truth when it pertains to emotional illness is difficult to bear, though insight into its implications provides a unique opportunity for adaptation and growth. Thus, the application of the insights contained in these pages may at times prove painful; in the long run, however, they can create coping capacities that are highly serviceable. This book is dedicated, then, not only to truth tellers and truth receivers, but also to those lie communicators who, in their inevitable struggle with life itself and emotional pain, come to these pages in the hope of finding a less costly way of being and adjusting.

PART I
ENCODING AND DECODING MESSAGES

CHAPTER 1

TWO FORMS
OF EXPRESSION

Of all of the marvels in human communication, perhaps the most awesome is the ability of the human mind to express itself simultaneously on two distinct and yet interconnected levels of meaning. And yet, this same organ can also express itself in singular, direct fashion without a trace of a significant second meaning. Well beyond any measure of conscious control, the mind shifts automatically and almost instinctively from one form of expression to the other, depending on its own psychophysiological state and on external conditions.

A PSYCHOLOGICAL PARADOX

This capacity to generate encoded messages with one surface meaning that simultaneously embodies a second, and disguised meaning, is highly adaptive. People find it unbearable to deal directly and consciously with terrifying emotional experiences and fantasies for very long. Such extended confrontations tend to fragment and even to annihilate their victims psychologically. Thus, coping through indirection is merciful and essential. Yet it can be carried too far. The very communicative defenses that protect our sanity can cause madness: psychological functioning is filled with such paradoxes.

Because we deal with so much that is emotionally important through double or encoded messages, we must understand this remarkable process of camouflage. In the secrets of encoding lies the answer to the decoding process. Further, insight into both forms of communication—single and multiple message—can provide us with a unique and vitally important means of understanding ourselves and others.

ENCODING AS EMOTIONAL PROTECTION

As a rule, communication outside of awareness involves matters of grave concern. We tend to use encoded messages in the presence of danger from within ourselves or from others. It is under the most stressful conditions of living, then, that we use meaningful layered communication. Messages—direct and encoded—are responses to external (and internal) stimuli. They are complex, adaptive reactions fraught with both meaning and actual consequences.

We send a wide variety of encoded communications. Well beyond our direct awareness, we take threatening, unconsciously registered perceptions and daydreams (or fantasies) and forge them into poems and stories, dreams and symptoms, unexpected accidents and uncharacteristic behaviors, and even into such acts of violence as murder and suicide. Thus it is often critical that we recognize the traumatic situations which prompt ourselves and others to communicate through indirect and encoded expressions. Often we exhibit early warning signs in relatively harmless forms: a day- or night dream, an innocuous but unexpected action, a slip of the tongue, or a not-too-painful symptom. If we learn how to decode the triggers of such messages, we may then be in a position to comprehend and reduce the pain of our hidden, inner needs and our disturbing perceptions of others. If we fail at this type of decoding, often we are rendered vulnerable to new symptoms and dangerous actions. Decoding in terms of evocative stimuli is the most critical means available to us for the understanding of the unconscious part of the mind.

TWO ILLUSTRATIONS

To offer a rather commonplace example, we may consider an incident between Paul and his wife, Rose. One evening Paul comes home from work to find Rose in the kitchen, depressed and irritable from a violent headache. Without warning, Paul furiously attacks his wife, complaining that she is always sick, always complaining, and never there when he needs her. An extended argument ensues.

From this brief description, some people might say that Paul is hostile and suffers from unresolved aggression. For us, these *inferences* are so general and intellectualized as to constitute virtually meaningless clichés. For a far more subtle appreciation of Paul's behavior, we need to know its trigger. On that basis, his reaction to his wife could be understood and *decoded* as a specific, encoded message.

Thus suppose we were to learn that Paul and Rose had been married for five years and that Paul very much wanted Rose to have his baby but that their efforts at conception had been unsuccessful. Preliminary tests have indicated that a pelvic infection Rose had suffered some years earlier is their major difficulty. Beyond that, Rose has behaved on the surface as if she wanted to get pregnant, although she has often avoided intercourse when she was probably ovulating. Although neither Paul nor Rose had consciously recognized her reluctance, these tendencies had registered in Paul unconsciously as encoded and unrecognized perceptions of his wife.

The immediate trigger for Paul's outburst at his wife had come earlier that afternoon when she had mentioned on the telephone that she had just begun to menstruate. In light of this trigger, Paul's behavior could be seen to have the following unconscious meanings: (1) His manifest complaint that his wife is ill all the time can be taken as an encoded message that because of her pelvic infection she has not been able to conceive; (2) Paul's fury can be understood as an encoded enactment of his unconscious fantasy that by menstruating, his wife is destroying their fetus. (His unconscious, though mistaken, belief—and wish—was that his wife conceived each month but could not maintain the pregnancy.); and (3) Paul's attack on Rose was also an attack on himself, given his unconscious fantasy that despite the medical findings, Paul himself was responsible for their infertility, himself physically defective.

As we can see, if Paul had been capable of decoding a variety of communications he generated both to himself and to his wife in light of the issues disturbing him (in essence, if Paul were capable of *trigger decoding*), he could have understood the sources and influence of his anger and guilt about his wife's inability to become pregnant. He could then have modulated or resolved his hostility toward himself and his wife. As a bonus, he would also soon have realized that Rose's headache was itself a physical expression of an encoded message of her own, in all probability an expression of her own rage at both of them at her failure to become pregnant. Clearly, trigger decoding would have provided Paul with a unique perspective on the situation.

Of course, not all encoded messages involve verbal attacks and painful somatic symptoms. Both traumatic and highly gratifying experiences can trigger positive, loving encoded expressions, including efforts to help those who have hurt us or who wish to love us.

The encoded expression of rageful fantasies and perceptions may actually prove life-threatening. For example, Susan and her mother live alone. One night her mother attempts suicide with an overdose of sleeping pills. She had told Susan of her suicidal feelings, and her daughter had implored her to obtain psychiatric help and to provide assurances that she would not actually attempt to kill herself. All of this was to no avail.

Susan's conscious reaction upon discovering her mother in a comatose state was one of grave concern and upset. She felt greatly worried and even somewhat consciously guilty for somehow failing her mother. Still she arranged for her mother's medical care and hospitalization and maintained her composure throughout the experience.

Nonetheless, on the day after the suicide attempt and after visiting her mother in the hospital, while driving home Susan failed to see a stop sign at a familiar corner near her house. She smashed headlong into another car, nearly killing herself and the other driver. The accident, as we shall see, was Susan's encoded expression of a variety of unconscious images.

Entirely outside of her awareness, Susan had found a devastating way of communicating a series of encoded reactions to her mother's suicide attempt. First, the accident expressed

Susan's rage at her mother for having ignored Susan's pleas that she find psychiatric help and not attempt to kill herself. Second, the accident expressed Susan's identification with her mother and with her mother's suicide attempt. It communicated her murderous rage at her mother for trying to take her own life. It also communicated Susan's murderous rage at herself for having somehow failed her mother and her belief (in part unconscious and valid) that she had contributed to the suicide attempt. Finally, the accident expressed Susan's unrecognized rage at her father. He had recently left her mother, thereby triggering her mother's suicide attempt, itself filled with encoded messages expressed in a highly destructive fashion.

Had Susan decoded her mother's hidden messages before the suicide attempt, she might have handled the problem more sensitively, and the suicide attempt might have been prevented. Had Susan begun to decode her own self-directed but disguised messages (on the night of her mother's suicide attempt, for instance, Susan had dreamt of a young girl who killed her mother and then herself), she might have prevented her accident. With better control, resources, and understanding, Susan might have been able to express her outrage, guilt, and self-hatred through day- and night dreams rather than through a life-threatening accident.

SOME HISTORICAL PERSPECTIVES

This book is dedicated to illuminating how we encode messages of the kind expressed by Paul and Susan and her mother. Historically, it was Sigmund Freud, in his greatest expression of genius, *The Interpretation of Dreams* (1900), who first described how the unconscious mind creates and sends messages. Freud's efforts began with a single, highly charged dream, the Irma dream, which became the first dream specimen of psychoanalysis. Dreamt in July of 1895, at a time of considerable personal and professional duress, the dream prompted an extended series of associations from Freud. Irma was both a friend and patient of Freud and the dream involved an examination of her mouth and indications that she had been made ill through a contaminated injection of toxins that would soon be eliminated through some form of dysentery. By studying the manifest dream and his responsive associations, Freud unraveled how we both disguise or avoid and yet express issues which plague us emotionally. Surprisingly, Freud also found that the strange form of thinking that is the basis for the creation of dreams and all other forms of unconscious communication is also the mechanism by which emotional symptoms are developed. In other words, emotional disorders are a form of unconscious communication, and they, like dreams, have two levels of representation. They do not resemble simple, logical thought.

ANALYZING EMOTIONAL TRIGGERS

Recent studies of the encoding and decoding processes have developed out of Freud's early decoding methods. One such method of understanding the hidden meanings in a dream is to analyze the dream's *day residue* (its daytime stimulus or trigger). This method replaces the more intellectualized and clichéd translations of encoded messages with formulations that are lively, full of emotional impact, and deeply personal.

By studying how a given person deals with emotional triggers it is possible to identify two basic *styles of communicating*. In the first, the individual responds to an emotionally laden experience with expressions of truths. In the second, however, these truths are obliterated and fictions substituted. We can gain many important insights once we make this distinction about styles of communicating.

Thus by reaching back to Freud and his explanations of unconscious processes and by developing new distinctions about how people communicate, we can contribute to the age-old attempt to understand how human beings function, adapt, and express their deepest feelings.

CHAPTER 2

PERSPECTIVES ON HUMAN COMMUNICATION

Whether it is a dream, a presidential address, or intimate words of affection, there is a sender, a receiver, and a message. Together, they form a communicative unit. The sender intends to convey a particular message, though often much of what he or she has conveyed is well beyond his or her direct awareness. The message itself may be in keeping with conscious intentions or at considerable variance with them. The receiver also registers a particular conscious meaning yet often receives far more unconscious meaning.

On the face of it, the likelihood of error or distortion in communication is considerable. This very exposition is offered with the acknowledged risk of communicative misunderstanding. Given the complexities, it is a wonder that so often people can agree on what their communications do mean. Total confusion would seem the more likely outcome.

It is a special and important quality of the human mind that a vast portion of its psychological operations take place unconsciously. There is virtually no way we can be aware of the existence of some of these unconscious processes. Others, especially as they involve disguised or unconscious messages, are revealed because they find some measure of compromised expression. Much of our information, perception, imagination, much of what is essentially human, is expressed unconsciously and in encoded fashion. One of the great misfortunes of psychic structure is that our mind's enormous unconscious resources are often unavailable to our conscious understanding for use in our daily functioning. In this book, we will be dealing not with mysterious psychophysiological forces, but with unconscious thinking and functioning as they are revealed through compromise and disguise.

COMMUNICATION AS ESSENTIAL TO SURVIVAL

Communicative exchanges give substance to our lives; they are essential for survival and growth. We know that we require a sufficient amount of internal communication, as in private thoughts, fantasies, and dreams, to maintain our sanity. The need for expression is powerful in all human beings, although often it is compromised by strong needs for defense, non-communication, and withdrawal. Self-expression is important to all coping efforts and especially so in emotionally trying situations. Interpersonally, the inherent danger of direct expression of highly charged perceptions and fantasies for both the sender and the receiver—the fear of an assault of primitive bluntness—leads to the compromise formation of encoded messages. Still, messages of this kind, imaginatively disguised, constitute our finest moments of creativity, discovery, and maturation. At the same time, they are also an essential part of that which is most base and disturbed in each of us.

TWO PARABLES OF COMMUNICATION

From the very dawn of humankind, there have been efforts at expression, however crude. Long before the development of language, individuals conveyed messages without words, through sounds, posture, and gestures. In time, there was pictorial representation and a flowering of signs and symbols. With language came the written word and very precise messages as well as more abstract and imaginative creations. As the human mind evolved, it developed the capacity for automatic disguise, and hidden messages became part of our repertory of expressions.

These historical developments evidently took place in the face of considerable conflict. Some of this conflict is recorded in the biblical story of the Tower of Babel. The story tells how at the time, humankind possessed a single, precise language.

When the people sought to know more about themselves and their God, they built a tower toward heaven. But their thirst for expression and knowledge was seen as excessive and sinful by God. His secrets were not to be captured or revealed. The tower was destroyed, and the people who had come together were dispersed. Their single universal language was transformed into a multitude of tongues. Messages were no longer communal and readily understood and shared. They required translation, decoding. With so many forms of expression, humankind was at odds with itself.

By cautiously applying a kind of decoding effort to this parable, we see that it appears to portray the pain and guilt involved in the pursuit of self-knowledge. It contains a warning that it is dangerous to communicate too openly and directly. Its encoded message may well be that it is necessary for human beings to disguise and encode their messages to protect themselves and others. The tale portrays the quest for truth and understanding as perilous. Too much insight brings down the heavens.

Another biblical story portrays the dangers of too much knowledge. However, it promises as well great rewards for those with the courage of foresight. This is the well-known tale of Joseph and his brothers. Joseph's downfall begins with his prophetic dream that his own sheaves of wheat would stand erect and his brothers' sheaves would bow before them. Without a knowledge of the trigger for this ancient dream, we may apply a general method of symbolic decoding. Joseph's pride in his capacity for prophecy (insight) is easily deciphered from this dream message. Its communication to his brothers leads to his near murder and eventual exile.

Later Joseph hears the pharaoh's dreams. Seven lean cows devour seven who are fat, and seven thin ears of corn swallow up seven full ears. The challenge to the populace is to decipher the disguised prophecy in these two dreams. Only Joseph, after all his suffering, rightly understands them as predicting seven years of plenty followed by seven years of famine. His symbolic decoding places Joseph in a favored position, and he goes on to right the harm that had been done to him.

The veiled message in the story of Joseph has two layers. Those who boldly express hidden messages filled with self-aggrandizement or hostility may come to grief. Better to withhold such messages or to be more obscure. But the second layer of meaning is that those select persons who hold the key to the mysteries of human expression shall be richly rewarded as prophets and sages, even in their own time. The tale, then, expresses both the dangers and the special compensations inherent in such wisdom.

THE HUMAN CHILD AS COMMUNICATOR

Every human being recapitulates in his or her own special way the history of humankind's communicative development. At the very moment of birth, the infant makes use of crude but budding abilities to relate to others and to express himself or herself. Some measure of internal communication and a full communicative link to the mother are essential for the continuation of life itself.

The infant functions as both sender and receiver. His or her messages, like those of early humans, are nonverbal. At times they are difficult to decode. They are expressed through noises and physical movements, through sometimes stormy showers of emotion, and they are conveyed in a broad and global manner. The infant's clearest messages tend to involve basic needs for nutrition and caring. We are all familiar with the cry of a hungry infant, and the sometimes more agitated cry of a soiled baby in need of changing.

There are broad individual differences in the communicative range and styles of infants. Despite their psychophysiological limitations, they are as a group able to express a remarkably wide assortment of messages. Such messages are a problem to decipher, not so much because they reflect the use of an unconscious encoding process, but mainly because of their crudeness. The needy infant may whine and cry and cling to his or her mother. However, the same behavior may arise from hunger pains, bowel cramps, or an open diaper pin.

As the infant develops there is a broadening of communicative range and a refinement of communicative tools. Not only do words and full language develop, but the child grows more sophisticated in the use of physical and other nonverbal messages. Even silences take on more definitive meaning. The previously nondescript flailing and crying shifts to a specific pointing to sources of discomfort and soon there is the use of words with which to convey even more definitive messages.

SINGLE AND MULTIPLE MESSAGES

The child develops two simultaneous means of expression—multi-leveled and discrete (singular or separate). In the latter form, the child's messages become sharper, more explicit and direct, and they more accurately portray his or her intentions. The logic and realistic utility of the messages improve. These qualities enhance not only the child's relatively concrete and direct messages, but also form the basis for the use of abstractions, generalizations, and more broadly, deliberately invoked signs and symbols. The repertoire of direct, adaptive, reality-oriented communication is enormously expanded.

As we know, an infant lacks the capability of pinpointing his or her sources of need and discomfort. Messages are self-oriented, and there is little that reflects concern for others. As specificity improves, the child is able to more definitively express his or her wishes in respect to not only the general matter of basic needs such as those reflected in hunger, but also in regard to specific culinary and other less crucial preferences. However, it requires considerably more development to make shifts such as those that involve realizations of classes of individuals and objects, such as men, women, dogs, cats, chairs, and the rest. In addition, the coping ability reflected in a child's messages improves considerably over time—compare for example, his or her early ill-defined tantrum to the specific request for aspirin because of a headache.

In the use of multi-leveled messages, the child at first develops a capacity for deliberate concealment and disguise. Afraid to ask directly for a bar of candy, he or she talks about having run errands, having been so good, and wishing for a reward. Quite consciously, the individual learns how to use implication rather than straightforward messages. In many instances, this new capacity is quite adaptive. Instead of an outraged parent refusing a direct request for a new bike, there may be the considerate parent who listens to the child's allusions to his or her friend's new two-wheeler, the hope to be able to ride a bike to school, and similar indirect messages.

In the extreme, the child finally learns how to lie, to deliberately falsify a given message. Often, complementary messages contain the falsehood in encoded form. In the accusation that a sibling has taken money from their father's wallet may lie the guilty confession of an errant youngster. Lies, too, are used in the service of coping, though they may wreak havoc with sender and receiver alike.

Simultaneously with the development of deliberate encoding, there is the origin and enhancement of a capacity to automatically and unconsciously encode dangerous raw messages—both dangerous perceptions and disturbing fantasies. The child becomes capable of expressing multiple levels of meaning, doing so without conscious intention. Under emotional stress, in dreams, and in the psychotherapeutic setting, a person is especially likely to use this type of communication. It also appears in private forms of play and fantasy, relieving tension as it fosters the compromise between expressed meaning and defense. All forms of creativity involve an exquisite mixture of direct and indirect communication.

Many facets of these developments are reflected in the dreams of children. At first, they are entirely absent. Next, they tend to be rather simple and concrete. They usually reflect basic needs, as seen in a dream of eating an ice cream sundae or taking a pleasure trip with the family. Still later, however, there is a sense of complexity as the child begins to dream of issues that lie beyond his or her basic needs, such as matters of rivalry, hostility, and the many other aspects of more mature inner and interpersonal struggles and satisfactions. The simple dream of eating an ice cream sundae becomes a complex dream of being in a strange ice cream parlor, of taking the sundae away from a young child who looks like the dreamer's brother, and of escaping from the store owner who is in pursuit of the dreamer with a knife. Through seemingly innocent associations to the dream, a sensitive listener can detect underlying messages that involve sibling rivalry, bodily anxieties, fearful images of the father, murderous hostility toward both the parents and sibling, and other such concealed but partially expressed messages.

THE IDEAL MIXTURE

Messages that are heavily laden with single, surface implications and relatively barren of underlying meaning tend to be dull, empty, and lifeless. They have utility but little else. They are of minimal interest, as seen in a mother's request for a child to buy six items at the local supermarket and in the messages involved in learning to do arithmetic or how to spell. There is little to stimulate the imagination. Still, there is an endless array of this type of message unit, vital for our survival though concrete and simplistic.

On the other hand, messages with too little surface meaning tend to appear idiosyncratic, unintelligible, or sick. Should someone state that there is a half-moon on Tenth Avenue while the deer and the antelope play, the message-receiver would feel confused and wonder about the mental state of the sender. An important requirement of both conscious and unconscious encoding is that its direct message be sensible while the hidden meanings are suitably disguised. In all, we find those messages that have imaginative surface implications and several levels of easily sensed (if difficult to define) underlying encoded meanings especially exciting and provocative. Therein lies the beauty of a poem or a novel, and of an exquisite and unforgettable moment of love.

CHAPTER 3
SURFACE MESSAGES

While, as noted, surface messages tend to be flat, dull, and often simply utilitarian, we must begin there before moving into more mysterious realms. We must establish a sound foundation for our exploration of the encoding and decoding processes by developing a reliable sense of single-message expressions, their properties and uses. This effort will also help us to eventually distinguish those messages with essentially one (surface) meaning from those, often of similar appearance, with multiple implications.

SOME WORD DERIVATIONS

The dictionary indicates that the basic element in the word *message* is "mess." *Message* stems from the Latin word *missus*, which is a course at a meal; and from *mittre*, which means to put, send, or smite. The word *mess* alludes to a quantity of food and to a group of persons who regularly take their meals together ("messmates"). It also refers to the place where such meals are served (as in "mess hall"). A rather different usage for the word *mess* involves a confused, dirty, or offensive state or condition—a jumble, a blunder, a misunderstanding, or the consequences of misconduct. As a verb, *mess* implies both supplying with meals and making dirty or untidy. It also suggests disarranging, bungling, manhandling, playing with, and interfering or meddling.

In our brief study of the development of communication, we identified a conflict between expression and defense, meaning and nonmeaning or confusion. We saw too that messages could be used to satisfy the most basic needs for both nurture and aggression. These characteristics are embodied in the origins of this word. The derivation of the word *message* contains feeding and sustaining qualities and also reflects the potential for hurtfulness and confusion (for smiting or throwing missiles). The inherent tendency defensively to disarrange and encode messages—to jumble them—is also implied.

The related word, *communicate*, on the other hand, implies only revelation, making known, and the passing on of information and knowledge. Its roots are in the Latin word for imparting, participating, having in common, and possessing meaning. To communicate emphasizes the qualities of sharing and transmission, as its related words—communion, communism, and community—show. *Communication* therefore shares the positive, nurturant, and informing qualities of *message* and lacks its dirty and hostile qualities.

A MESSAGE VERSUS A COMMUNICATION

These two definitions lead us to an important distinction: that between communication (in which relating, signifying, and defining are inherent) and messages (which may or may not possess these qualities). Messages, we are warned, may be designed to foul up or destroy both meaning and relatedness. This distinction lets us avoid the erroneous but common assumption that everything an individual expresses is designed for positive communication.

THE MESSAGE IN ISOLATION

Isolated messages tend to be highly complex and to contain a multiple of attributes. At face value, it is usually impossible to tell whether we are dealing with a single- or multiple-meaning message. While this distinction will ultimately be of considerable importance to us, it will be helpful first to generate a sense of the nature of surface messages themselves. The following illustrates three among the almost infinite variety of messages:

> Ship these books to Chicago.
>
> If you don't get these books off to Chicago, I'm going to cut your throat.
>
> I was cutting this man's throat because he wouldn't ship these books to Chicago.

Messages in *isolation* may appear straightforward or inherently ambiguous. We need some larger context to settle the immediate questions we might raise. At the very least, we require some information about the sender of the message, its intended receiver, the setting in which it is conveyed, and even the form the message takes. Messages may be clear or unclear, cold or warmly emotional. They may be informative, imaginative, helpful, constructive, truthful, and false. They may express feelings or serve an endless number of purposes. They may exist as everyday statements, dreams, fantasies, and even be entirely visual rather than verbal.

For example, a threat to cut someone's throat if he or she does not get some books shipped off to Chicago may be quite real or used for its symbolic implications and its power to generate in the receiver both emotion and action. There is little way of knowing because of a critical lack of context. At the very least, we would like to know whether the sender of this message is holding a knife or smiling.

In all, the surface of a message provides only a limited amount of information. Often, the most important dimensions of a message require additional information, such as context, setting, the relationship involved, and sometimes the associations of the sender and even of the receiver.

A similar problem arises from the third statement, the message about actually having cut the man's throat because he would not ship the books to Chicago. We would hope the statement came from a dream rather than from testimony at a murder trial. Still, without its context, we simply do not know how to understand its direct meaning, nor can we determine any hidden or latent implications.

Thus, the surface of a message contains its manifest or direct meanings. As we have seen, the definition of these meanings may be straightforward or require an appreciation of the total context within which the message has been sent. Still, we make use of the term *manifest contents* to refer to all evident and surface meanings of a message. As already indicated, there are many messages whose implications are restricted to this level of expression. On the other hand, there are many messages that involve both surface and deeper meanings, manifest and *latent contents* and implications. These deeper meanings are expressed indirectly through the surface message and are disguised in some form in its manifest elements. They are detectable through a full appreciation of the total context of the message, though they often require the specific associations of the message sender. In general, there is some degree of communality between the manifest theme and a latent theme: the direct message bears some resemblance to the hidden expression. For these multi-leveled messages, the manifest expression contains in some disguised form the latent meaning; there is both positive communication and defensive disguise.

For us, the attributes of the surface of messages is of interest, though of minor importance. As we familiarize ourselves with such attributes, we will concern ourselves as well with the more important question of whether a particular surface message is of single or multiple implications. We will also begin to develop the distinctions between manifest and latent message contents, preparing the way for a later study of the means by which we encode latent messages into manifest expressions.

Even on the surface, the first message, "Ship these books to Chicago," may not be as simple as it seems. If it came from the shipping manager of a book publisher, it would be a mundane instruction. But what if these were the words of the retired shipping manager, sitting alone in his apartment, hallucinating about being back at the job? We as receivers would have an entirely different impression.

In the main, then, we learn little of the subtleties of human communication through an examination of messages in isolation. Without knowing their context, it is also impossible to tell whether we are dealing with a flat, linear message with a single meaning, or an encoded message with two or more meanings.

THE ROLE OF CONTEXT

Messages do not exist in limbo. They are always embedded in a *context* or framework, a setting or relationship, even if that context is within ourselves. The context provides perspective, confirms the meaning of simple messages, and somewhat illuminates complicated messages. The context also helps us to establish the important distinction, in most instances, between a realistic, solution-providing message and one that is quite unrealistic and a matter of either fantasy or distortion.

In order to offer a sensible discussion, it was necessary in the previous section to allude to possible contexts for each of these messages. Certainly, the impact of a message that someone intends to cut another person's throat would be rather different if it is a line from a play (a special space for messages of a particular kind), the threat of a nasty boss, the joke of a kind shipping manager, or the confused words of a knife-wielding hood. By knowing the relationship between a manifest message and its context, we can draw a reliable meaning from most messages.

Context includes not only attributes of the sender and receiver of the message, but also the entire history of their relationship and the nature of the setting in which the communication takes place. When a message is discordant with its context (e.g., when the shipping instructions are shouted out by an old man in an empty room), we think of it as unrealistic and fantasied. Depending on other contextual qualities, we may consider it to be a reflection of emotional illness. In general, under conditions of everyday life, a discrepancy between a manifest message and its context is indeed a sign of emotional disturbance. It is therefore of considerable importance to recognize the power that context has to change the constellation of meanings for even the simplest message.

MESSAGE FORMS

Messages of course are carried by such diverse vehicles as declarative statements, products of fantasy, the written word, all types of behavior, affects and emotions, body language, and even symptoms. A commonly used distinction is that between verbal and nonverbal messages. An equally important distinction separates intellectualized thoughts from emotionally charged images.

Nonverbal messages tend to be somewhat ambiguous. They are often used as a means of conveying hidden or unconscious thoughts and feelings. While verbal messages are sometimes (though not always) highly intellectual and rational, nonverbal messages typically stir us outside our immediate awareness. They draw upon elusive unconscious processes and, with certain exceptions, tend to be vaguer and more global than verbal messages.

Take, for example, a situation in which Ted complains of a headache. He reports the headache verbally, but the headache itself is a nonverbal communication. Its most evident meaning is that Ted is suffering pain. Nonetheless, his headache may well be a result of, and therefore express, a number of fantasies outside of Ted's awareness. In order to ascertain the nature of these hidden fantasies, we would require Ted to speak with us rather freely, somewhat approaching the free associations of psychoanalysis.

For example, suppose Ted's thoughts drifted to his boss who had called him stupid and had assaulted him verbally. If Ted then produced an image of puncturing a balloon with a pin, we would have some reason to propose that Ted's headache was based on his conscious and unconscious perception of the boss's assault on his (Ted's) mind. We might propose that the headache also represented Ted's unconscious fantasy (wish) of attacking his boss in kind. Consciously, Ted had no direct thought of revenge. These wishes were expressed in encoded form through his symptom.

Messages, then, are expressed in a wide range of forms. Some surface meanings are clear, others ambiguous. A study of nonverbal messages suggests that many can be reduced to hidden or unconscious fantasies and perceptions. Physical symptoms, therefore, are often double messages: on the surface they speak of pain and discomfort; underneath they express hidden wishes.

THE MOTIVES BEHIND MESSAGES

Messages are generated for specific reasons and needs. They are directed toward particular goals and accomplishments. Motives are part of the context of messages. They help to shape their form and content. They may reflect inner need—psychological, physical, or both (psychophysiological) —or the requirements of a particular relationship or other outer reality. The stimuli for messages are therefore both internal and external. In general, inner and outer need systems tend to act in coordinate fashion, though in most emotionally laden situations it is the disturbing outer precipitant which has the greatest influence on the exchange of messages that follows. Messages are generated, then, to deal with inner and outer problems which require or demand solution. They may serve the sender quite well and relieve tensions, or they may fail entirely.

Messages may have clear purpose or appear random and without deliberate intention. In the latter circumstances, we assume the presence of a hidden agenda, an unconscious motive. It seems safe to assume that every message, no matter how seemingly nonsensical and unrelated to adaptive tasks, has a purpose and function, if only to reflect and deal with an inner need.

INNER- AND OUTER-DIRECTED MESSAGES

Messages may be directed to others or form part of an *internal dialogue*. Privately, we send and receive messages in a near-continuous stream. They take the form of discrete thoughts, various images, perceptions, dreams, and such. They are part of our everyday efforts at coping.

In the messages above about sending books to Chicago, the instruction to ship the books serves a practical purpose which meets a number of evident, realistic, and internal needs for the sender. The message which contains the throat-cutting threat may well be designed with a similar realistic need in mind (i.e., to get the books off to Chicago), though the threat suggests as well that the message serves in significant fashion to communicate and satisfy certain sadistic needs within the sender. Should the message denote an actual assault on its receiver, its purpose would have become murder and the inner need one of uncontrolled violence.

Ambiguous messages, whose motivation and purpose are uncertain, tend to confuse and put off the receiver. We realize, then, that some messages bring the sender and receiver closer and into greater harmony—they create *communicative closeness*. Other messages generate feelings of distance and non-communication—they lead to *communicative alienation*. The presence or absence of evident surface meaning and function in a message, then, greatly influence not only the degree of understanding of the message, but also the nature of the relationship between the sender and the receiver.

THE PRESENCE OF MEANING IN MESSAGES ───────

The issue of whether messages are meaningful is not as simple as it might seem. There are often problems in reaching a consensus on this issue. Some of these problems depend on the knowledge of the different receivers of a particular communication, while at other times the ambiguity of the message itself is the critical factor. In matters of this kind, it is essential to have a means by which an individual can validate or verify his or her judgment regarding the meanings involved (see below).

As for meaning itself, there is the *inherent meaning* of the message per se. There is also the *contextual meaning*, the implications of the factors which surround the discrete message. Many messages have *commonsense meaning* and deal with the pleasures and drudgery of everyday life. Others have *technical meaning* and require special knowledge or information (such as computer science or even psychoanalysis). Finally, some messages have *personal meaning* which may relate to widely shared experiences or to singular experiences—containing much meaning for the sender though little for the receiver.

In general, meaningful messages promote communicative closeness, while those that are meaningless create communicative distance. Meaningless messages tend to confuse and interfere with relatedness; they are often experienced as hostile and provocative.

TRUE AND FALSE MESSAGES

A meaningful message is not necessarily true. Many meaningful statements are quite false. It is, for example, meaningful to state that the sun will rise in the west, although if we check this statement against observable fact, we discover that it is false.

In general, a message's truthfulness is the extent to which it is faithful to inner and outer reality. Of course, it is possible to create statements that are true for some individuals and not for others—e.g., the comment that people react with open emotions when hurt.

Attempting to determine the extent to which a surface message reflects the truth raises many complex issues. Some messages relate to easily verified facts. For others, such as those messages which involve technical matters (those made by scientists about the nature of the atom, for example), we must rely heavily on others for validation.

A different set of difficulties arise when someone tells us that he or she is feeling sad or angry or even that he or she had a fanciful daydream about a plane trip to Chicago. Although there are some surface clues to a person's private feelings and fantasies, these are extremely limited. Much of our understanding will therefore depend on a sampling of a sequence of messages to check for internal consistency and accumulation of evidence. We would then pay attention to the context of the message as well as to the general credibility of the sender. Finally, by detecting any encoded messages in the manifest sequence of communications, we could compare manifest and latent contents to determine the truthfulness of the surface expressions.

Even internal messages create moments of uncertainty. We feel a pain somewhere in our stomach, but are we correct in assuming it is a bowel cramp rather than a gall bladder attack? For another example, are we truthful about our feelings toward our boss? We are certainly capable of consciously and yet unwittingly lying to ourselves. In a nutshell, then, every message, whatever its source, requires a careful determination of its true and false manifest qualities.

The degree of truthfulness of a manifest message strongly affects its impact. Truthful messages permit a sense of certainty in the receiver; false messages virtually always create communicative estrangement and a sense of having been provoked. Even when provocative, truthful messages are in general rather adaptive. However, truth may at times be an expression of hostility and may even serve to inappropriately avoid other, more compelling truths that the sender does not wish to deal with or acknowledge. Thus, even truthful messages may be utilized in maladaptive and inappropriate ways. Here too, we require an understanding of the total context of a message in order to specify its functions and attributes.

A young man expresses his love for a young woman. She will feel secure in regard to the meaning of this message and her relationship with him when there is a background of affection and commitment. On the other hand, the same message would provoke a considerable degree of uncertainty if it were generated soon after the young man had been seen in the company of a different woman. In the latter situation, the contradiction in expressed messages (words and behavior) creates not only a sense of mistrust, but also one of bewilderment.

Lies are inherently self-gratifying and tend to interfere with relatedness and problem solving. They tend to be attempts at coping through magically falsifying some aspect of consensually validated reality. As such, the lie is often a sign of coping failure and psychopathology. Despite that, because of its exquisite power, its possible function as a source of immediate relief and triumph, and its use as a means of dismissing a problem, the lie is often greatly valued (consciously or unconsciously), and the liar frequently glorified. Since the truth can be piercing and painful, lies are often used as a means of obtaining immediate relief from this pain. As we proceed, much that applies to surface lies (deliberate or inadvertent) will also apply to unconscious lies—falsifications beyond the awareness of the sender and sometimes of the receiver as well. We will soon turn to the entire issue of the truth and falseness of both manifest and latent messages.

VALIDATION

It appears, then, that such important attributes of manifest messages as their purpose, meaning, and veracity require standards for their evaluation. Different people listening to the same message may come to remarkably dissimilar conclusions. Often the issue of validation is set aside, and the situation becomes one of personal bias and even autocracy. Some type of consensus on these basic aspects of surface messages is necessary for individual functioning as well as for all forms of social interaction. It is necessary to overcome the human tendency to accept automatic impressions with little reflective thought. Otherwise one is left with anarchy, uncertainty, and chaos, with each person living in his or her own little world of unconfirmed impressions and beliefs.

There are at least three means of verifying the avowed implications of *manifest* messages. The goal of verification is the correct identification of the sender's intentions as well as the receiver's impressions. This process stands in contrast to that involved in validating *encoded* messages. There the intentions of the sender are unconsciously expressed and therefore inherently valid, and validation centers around determinations arrived at through the decoding method of the receiver.

The following are the main methods of validating one's impressions of manifest messages:

THE SCIENTIFIC METHOD

This type of verification makes use of principles of logic and observation and is based on methods that can be replicated by others. It employs empirical tests—field tests, so to speak —in which matters of evidence, testing, prediction, and replication of outcome all play a role. It is a way of developing standards of confirmed reality and truth that can be systematically reaffirmed and used by others. Through repeated testing, we eventually establish a body of accepted knowledge and facts and a measure of communality regarding the implications of certain types of typical messages.

There is a tendency to idealize the scientific method, and because of this, its limitations must be recognized. The scientific approach depends upon tools of testing and observation which tend to evolve in the direction of greater precision. Truth is always relative to the instruments by which it is measured. Some of today's facts will be tomorrow's misconceptions.

In everyday life, often in relatively simple ways, we make considerable use of this method of validation. If the shipping manager says, "Ship these fifty books to Chicago," the clerk might count the books in the carton and check the address label. If the shipping manager's face flushed when he spoke of wanting to cut the other person's throat, we might assume the speaker was angry and attempt to validate our assumption by noting such measures as an increase in his pulse, the degree of redness in his face, or the intensity of the aggressive tone to his words. If we are able to predict certain kinds of subsequent behaviors or consequences, that too would have a scientific quality.

Anything that we can measure, use for prediction, and have others verify through specific tests falls into the scientific method's sphere of confirmation. Quite often, we carry out such measures quite automatically and without being aware of the steps involved. The scientific method works considerably better, however, with objects rather than people. Still, it is the most reliable means of assuring the proper understanding of a message.

CONSENSUAL VALIDATION

Another means of validating one's impression of a message is to compare it with someone else's. We can ask the sender of the message his conscious intention and check it against our own appraisal. We can also ask other receivers about their evaluations and compare them with our own. When there is essential agreement among observers, we have what is termed *consensual validation*.

With the scientific method, the controls and standards are carefully spelled out. Consensus, where we are dealing with two or more sets of subjective impressions, is less precise. Confined largely to the immediate present, this method is somewhat arbitrary and especially vulnerable to shared mis-perceptions and misconceptions. These drawbacks are all the more likely when there is a powerful need for conformity among the observers or where a single observer has undue influence over others. Consensual validation is also strongly affected by the fixed values, impressions, beliefs, accepted facts, general knowledge, and self-knowledge within the group.

For most surface messages consensual validation is easily obtained. Surface messages usually contain evident meanings of which the sender is likely to be aware and which one or more receivers are likely to detect quite readily and to agree upon. When disputes arise, one can turn for resolution to group discussion, to the development of a majority opinion, or to the more scientific forms of verification.

For example, two message receivers are likely to agree that there are ten cartons in a room, that it is now night time, and on other rather self-evident messages. On the other hand, if a sender states that he is not angry, the extent of agreement among message receivers will depend upon the confluence of additional evidence. In some situations, a consensus is readily achieved. While in others, there may be considerable dispute. It is here that the use of supplementary evidence may prove important, though often it is the dominant member of a pair of observers or a charismatic group leader whose opinion will hold sway. There is therefore a strong interplay between matters of evidence and those of personal influence. The more scientific the basis for consensus, the less important the personal factor.

SEEKING CONFLUENCE OF SUPPORTING EVIDENCE

As noted, groups or single observers may use this type of validation in regard to their impressions of messages. It is a way of checking one piece of evidence against other bits and pieces. We use it when we listen to a series of messages from a given sender or when we consider several qualities in a single message. Sometimes we develop a first impression and then check it against subsequent messages. We examine surface themes and see how well they connect. We incorporate sources of information from different kinds of messages—from words, affects, and bodily movements—and determine whether they support each other.

We used this type of verification in examining the shipping manager as he threatened to cut someone's throat for not sending some books to Chicago. Our hypothesis that the speaker was angry was validated by his hostile tone, pressured speech, clenched fists, the flush in his face, and by the tightness of his lips as he spoke. If his next sentence had been, "Damn it, there are times when I could really kill you," we would have further evidence of his anger. If, on the other hand, the next sentence had been, "How would you like to join me for dinner?" we would think that he is far less angry than our initial impression had led us to believe.

Other types of supportive evidence are derived from the context of the message. Thus, we usually seek a confluence of meaning in the communication itself and in the relationship and physical space in which it is set.

THE SUBJECTIVE FACTOR

In all efforts at validation, one must be open to the possible lack of support for one's impression of a given message. If one cannot validate one's impression, one must acknowledge this lack and reformulate. Because we tend to cling to our own impressions, subjecting them to skepticism will prove useful.

All efforts at validation involve a major subjective factor. The scientific method is designed to minimize subjectivity; consensual validation allows for more subjectivity. Even with conscious and direct messages, one can be so biased as to misinterpret an entire sequence of messages. In such a case, one is unlikely to be unaware of one's distortion. One may even seem idiosyncratic, bizarre, or paranoid to others. For this reason, we are well advised to use multiple means of validation and to use them often. However, in the course of everyday communication, we usually cannot stop to make time-consuming validations. Therefore we must learn to validate messages automatically, unconsciously, or fleetingly consciously.

CHAPTER 4

THINKING OUTSIDE OF AWARENESS

In looking at moments when one functions as the sender of a message, our concern will be far less with surface messages and far more with those that are encoded. Suffice it to say that a message sender is, as we have seen, motivated by a combination of inner and outer needs to communicate and is consciously preoccupied with how best to convey a particular, manifest message. Almost no one attempts to deliberately invoke or regulate the unconscious encoding process. Most exceptions are among poets and writers who place themselves in a communicative state that tends to favor a significant measure of encoded or unconscious communication as part of the conscious endeavor. Still, when they are selecting a particular phrase or sentence (message), their concern remains with the surface flow of the narrative. Their creativity appears to lie in an automatic and unconscious ability to bring to their work encoded and disguised messages that have special meaning to many others.

TWO TYPES OF MESSAGES

There is some confusion because of the general failure to realize that the human individual is by no means always engaged in conveying encoded messages. As we have already noted, the human mind is quite distinctive in being able to shift from single-meaning expression to multiple-meaning expression. While not every individual shifts back and forth neatly, we may nonetheless clarify the conditions under which it is most likely that a person will communicate in one or the other fashion.

Single-meaning communication is utilitarian, reality-oriented, primarily conscious, and directed toward external tasks; it is characteristic of waking life. Characterized by its contact with reality, its use of logic, the manner in which a particular message stands for itself alone (e.g., a car is a car and not in addition a symbol of a phallus or the maternal body), its discreteness, and its freedom from inherent contra-dictions, Freud (1900) termed this type of thinking *secondary-process thinking*. He indicated as well that it involves a capacity for delay and for the tolerance of frustration such that inner needs are not immediately discharged and messages are imparted with due control and good perspective on the context.

Freud felt that this type of communication developed after the more primitive *primary-process thinking*, which is quite different from this rather evident and more conscious way of functioning. By and large (though with important exceptions), our familiar way of thinking and communicating is conscious mentation, and a rather different mode of expression or menta-tion is characteristic of thinking and communication outside of awareness—i.e., of unconscious expression.

UNCONSCIOUS ENCODING

As we now know, unconscious encoding is one of the great achievements of the human mind. The entire process is auto-matic and takes place outside of the awareness of the encoder. It is almost reflexive and appears to serve mainly the dual purpose of coping with disturbing inner (intrapsychic) and external (interpersonal) experiences through a combination of positive expression and communication on the one hand, and defensive protection and restraint on the other.

In its essence, then, unconscious encoding is a means by which we develop a compromised, disguised response to an emotionally laden trigger (an immediately disturbing stimulus). A communication that contains an unconsciously encoded message has both a manifest content and a latent content. The former may be a dream or other expression with a surface theme or a series of conscious statements that convey a particular sequence of ideas and feelings, and which have, as a rule, their own set of intentions and meanings. Virtually always, the sender of such a message is aware only of his or her *conscious* intentions and meaning. There has been no deliberate effort at producing a double or multiple message, and no immediate awareness of the hidden meanings contained within (and beneath) the surface expression. Such realizations are possible only through an analysis of the message, an effort that can be successful only in light of its trigger and total context, and the personal associations (thoughts and feelings connected with the message) of the sender.

Virtually any type of anxiety or other disturbing affect, and any threatening raw image (perception of others or oneself, as well as fantasies and daydreams), will automatically prompt the invocation of unconscious encoding. This occurs whenever open and direct communication is perceived as dangerous internally and as a source of anxiety, or externally as a source of potential disturbance of an interpersonal relationship. Most of the time this very perception of the dangerous qualities of open communication is itself quite unconscious, and registered automatically within the mind in a manner that leads, again quite unwittingly, to the use of the encoding process.

Unconscious encoding is a basic coping device vital to the psychic functioning and even survival of each human being. Some persons are quite gifted in these efforts, which serve not only self-protective functions but also are an essential component of all forms of creativity. Then too, these efforts may be quite successful and more than adequate to handle the emotional threat contained in the situation, or they may fail abysmally. In the latter instance, the sender often develops emotional symptoms as a new and relatively maladaptive effort at compromise and coping (a symptom is indeed a form of encoded message). Other consequences of communicative failure include periods of mental disorganization, the experience of primitive and raw perceptions and fantasies that are no longer softened and instead, prove to be deeply disturbing, and the expression of blunt and offensive messages to others.

Unconscious encoding, then, is a critical human resource which may be utilized, like all of our adaptive capacities, quite successfully or rather poorly.

In general, we make use of secondary-process thinking in virtually all aspects of our daily lives. It is of untold value that we are able to express ourselves with single-minded clarity, without the clutter of all kinds of double meanings and hidden messages which would be likely to confound the receiver and to interfere with the usual tasks and happenings in our daily lives.

MECHANISMS OF PRIMARY PROCESS

Primary-process thinking is fluid and loose, geared to immediate discharge or satisfaction, and little tuned to logic or reality. It operates through five main mechanisms:

Condensation, through which a single image or thought may stand simultaneously for several images or thoughts. Thus the appearance of a car in a dream may stand for the car itself, someone else's car, another vehicle such as a boat or a plane, the body of one or more women, and a specific scene or incident. One can readily imagine the chaos that would occur if someone, while discussing buying a car, spoke of it in a way that implied all of these different meanings. We are fortunate that we can close off this kind of thinking when necessary. On the other hand, it is highly adaptive to be able to attempt to cope outside of awareness with five or ten different emotional problems through a single, elaborate image.

Displacement, through which one person, situation, or object is used to represent another. One car stands for a second, one face for another, an incident yesterday for one that took place years ago. Displacement is perhaps the key primary-process mechanism. It enables us to deal with emotional pain through indirection or allusion, sparing us much additional anxiety.

Symbolization, by which one item through its attributes signifies another. In its broadest sense, symbolization implies all means by which one image can represent another, although in its narrow sense it refers to objects and situations that are commonly used to represent highly personal yet universal matters such as parts of the body and aspects of sexuality and primitive aggression. Thus a car may symbolize the maternal body and a tree the paternal phallus.

Secondary revision is the means by which an encoded communication is modified so that on the surface it is part of a sensible and logical sequence. Thus if a dreamer wanted to represent through an encoded message a struggle against castration, he might dream of being at a lumber camp and trying to prevent someone from sawing down a tree. The same principle applies to encoded free associations in psychotherapy, where the mind unconsciously modifies the underlying representations enough so that a series of logical free associations follow one upon another.

Concerns for representability is a mechanism closely related to secondary revision and a broader means of stating the fundamental principle that the human mind attempts to shape a series of encoded messages into a surface communication that has the greatest possible surface logic and sensibility. For this last reason it is important to know when an individual is making use of multiple communication, because the surface message can be disarmingly logical and realistic.

It is difficult at first to imagine and comprehend this strange and fluid flow of ideas and images dominated by the primary-process mechanisms. Yet there is no doubt that a large proportion of our mental functioning takes place in just this way. Not only are dreams largely under the sway of this mode of thought, but also most responses to emotionally traumatic situations, most types of creativity, virtually all emotional and psychologically founded symptoms, and the communications from patients in psychotherapy (and sometimes even from their therapists). Certain drugs, especially those which alter one's state of consciousness, shift the human mind into this mode of thinking as well. There is strong evidence that in response to emotionally charged situations, these multiple messages are extremely adaptive; single-message expressions could not handle the rich variety of feelings aroused under these conditions. Striking too is the capacity in virtually all persons to shift from one mode of thought to the other as conditions and inner needs indicate which will prove more adaptive.

UNCONSCIOUS EXPRESSION IN A DREAM

Consider the following message:

BEN: I'm in an elevator. This attractive woman is there with me. She has a tall, slim plant in her arms. She asks me if I want to go to bed with her.

If the context for this message were a conversation between Ben and his friend, Clem, we would soon discover that Ben was telling his friend about an incident that had occurred on a recent business trip. In such a message, the elevator would represent an actual place. The woman would be a specific individual. The small plant would be just that, and her seductive query would have been pretty much as stated—though it might have had a number of important implications.

In contrast, if Ben were in psychotherapy and Clem his therapist, we would find Ben here reporting a dream. Suppose the elevator brings to mind his mother's pregnancy, the delivery of his sister, and other recollections of gestation and birth. We would then have reason to propose that the elevator represents the womb of Ben's mother. If, then, other associations led Ben to recall several concrete experiences which took place in elevators, including a time when he was involved in an elevator accident, the same dream element would be understood to represent through *condensation* all of these additional scenes and incidents and their meanings.

By the same token, the use of *displacement* would already be in evidence. The woman in the elevator could be viewed as a stand-in for, and therefore a displacement from, Ben's sister. As other women appeared in Ben's associations, they too would be represented by this single female.

Suppose Ben's associations to the tall plant held by the woman went first to a plant in the bedroom he shared for a time with his sister (this room, then, would also be represented by the elevator—showing the use of condensation, displacement, and symbolization in a single representation), and to a time that a woman caressed his genitals. The latter association would indicate that the tall plant symbolized Ben's penis, just as on a more abstract level, it could symbolize his relationship with his sister. There is a strong likelihood here of underlying sexual fantasies and experiences between Ben and his sister— all of these conveyed in disguised form in this dream.

Further, suppose the woman's invitation to go to bed reminded Ben of a different woman he had once met on a subway train who had refused his invitation to have a drink. In this instance there is evidence of further condensation (the elevator also stands for the subway car), of displacement (from the subway car to the elevator), and of representation—here by an opposite (Ben's rejection is changed into a direct seduction). Strange indeed is this type of thinking, primary-process thinking, where one image can stand for its contradiction. Marvelous too is the realization that this apparently logical dream contains in fluid and encoded form so many hidden messages.

Through the context and associations to a dream or any other single message we can identify some of its unconscious meanings. For purposes of simplification, we have here concentrated on *symbolic translations* and *inferences* rather than a more elaborate and specific decoding process based on the implications of the immediate trigger (day residue) for this dream. Our purpose has been to show the kind of general evidence that Freud invoked in defining unconscious expression.

THE MENTAL WORLD OUTSIDE OF OUR AWARENESS

There are different ways in which ideas, memories, perceptions, fantasies, and the like can exist outside of direct awareness. However, for each unconscious expression we usually have a bit of surface evidence that it has already been subjected to the primary-process mechanisms. We are dealing with lack of awareness, not with lack of evidence or expression.

First, there is a vast range of images and perceptions of which we are unaware at the moment but which we could readily call to mind, if we chose. Many years ago, Freud (1900) called these *preconscious thoughts*. They tend to be not heavily encoded or particularly threatening. They are outside of awareness for reasons of efficient mental functioning—the fact that we can be aware of only one thought or image at a time—and not for defensive or protective reasons. Thoughts which are too dangerous have been termed *dynamically unconscious thoughts*, and they are kept out of awareness by some defense, some active mental obstacle. Such thoughts and images are dangerous and cause anxiety. As a result, outside of awareness, exerting a continuous influence, and surfacing from time to time in our dreams and in other encoded communications, there exist a myriad of *repressed* (defensively disguised and forgotten) memories, fantasies, and perceptions of ourselves and others.

To cite an example, Dan finds his sister-in-law, Elly, sexually attractive. However, the least semblance of a sexual thought about her prompts intense anxiety and guilt. Soon, Dan experiences a daydream in which he rescues a strange and beautiful woman from a burning building. She desires him sexually, but he demurs, satisfied with his heroic deed.

Knowing the *trigger* for this particular fantasy (the attraction to Elly), we can suggest that the daydream is a rather successfully disguised fantasy of seducing his sister-in-law (the rescue from the burning building) and renouncing these wishes toward her (the refusal of sexual favors). The intensity of the sexual wish, as well as the anxiety and guilt, are portrayed through the flames. This automatically encoded message reflects both the underlying forbidden wish and the defenses erected against its expression—sexual contact is desexualized and transformed into a rescue. When it does emerge, it is ascribed to someone else and is repudiated.

Suppose that Dan also had perceived Elly acting seductively. In that case, the flames from which he rescues the woman would represent an encoded representation of Elly's expressed sexuality. A less symbolic and less disguised portrayal of this perception appears in the unidentified woman's sexual offer (here, mainly displacement is at work). If, for reasons of defense, Dan had not been aware of Elly's seductiveness, we would have here evidence of the registration of a *perception outside of awareness* which then found encoded expression in this particular daydream.

HYPNOTISM AND FREUDIAN SLIPS ———————————

Post-hypnotic suggestion is another way of providing evidence for the unconscious part of the mind. A hypnotist may suggest to a subject that once out of a hypnotic trance, should the hypnotist clap his hands, the subject should hop on his left foot three times. With the command in place, along with the directive to remember nothing of the hypnotic experience, the subject is awakened. When the signal is given, the subject hops. The hypnotist then asks the subject to explain his most peculiar behavior. The reply is usually a rationalization: his foot was tingling or he felt like letting go. There is no conscious awareness of the true basis for the behavior, an unconscious need planted in him by the hypnotist.

Slips of the tongue, so-called "Freudian slips," also suggest unconscious influence. To oversimplify, they may be seen as instances in which a particular repressed inner thought or feeling eludes its defense and breaks through into conscious awareness. A man says to his resistant girlfriend, "I must hate, I mean, have you." Here, his underlying hostility breaks through in raw form. Had he used an encoded message, he might have verbally attacked a woman coworker at his place of business. Through displacement, he would thereby have vented his rage at his girlfriend.

Other evidence for unconscious influence is formed in moments when we behave in ways that are entirely out of keeping with our conscious thoughts and intentions. There are symptomatic acts such as accidentally locking one's keys in a car or letting a pot burn on a stove. Such inadvertent incidents speak for some kind of unconscious disturbance. Each of these behaviors, since their surface meanings do not sufficiently account for them, must also reflect and contain an encoded message.

Perhaps the main implied message of this chapter is that we need to delve more deeply into how we encode messages. Let us proceed to do just that.

CHAPTER 5
CONSCIOUS ENCODING

DELIBERATE ENCODING

It is possible and sometimes necessary to consciously and deliberately encode a message. We tend to do so in a dangerous or troublesome situation where it seems inadvisable to express ourselves directly. Often, it is a matter of being diplomatic, sensitive, and considerate. There are some painful messages that are best expressed through indirection. A good communicator (message sender) is able to choose the right mode for the right moment.

This type of conscious encoding shades into the everyday use of signs and symbols as a basic part of accepted language. To the extent that they are used deliberately, these messages are, however, a product of surface encoding.

In our studies of surface messages to this point, we have been dealing with accepted meanings, with word usages that have seen subjected to consensual verification. We have been dealing with dictionary meanings, commonly accepted with little ambiguity. A good term for this level of communication is *verifiable definition or meaning*.

PET NAMES

In contrast, communication through *encoded meaning* may occur in a number of different forms. There is the personal encoding shared by two individuals, such as pet names which lovers develop for each other and which take on special and secret implications. Ted calls his girlfriend "Poopserkettle" and "Sugarbush." The first word does not exist in verifiable language and the second pair of words have no verifiable meaning in combination. Thus, the first encoded message involves an endearing phrase which acquires its special qualities from the tone and manner in which Ted uses it, as well as through an allusion to a particular kind of metal pot with symbolic meaning. This creates an endearing phrase which implies for Ted and his girlfriend that she is someone precious, whom he likes to hold and cuddle, and who at times is very much a hot and steaming number.

Then, too, "Sugarbush" refers to a sweetening substance and to a type of plant or shrub which is sometimes used in unconscious language to represent the female genitals. Ted has not chosen these words deliberately and consciously to convey his sense of his girlfriend's sweetness and his attraction to her sexually. Instead, he is attempting to encode feelings of endearment which contain within them rather subtle innuendos of a sexual nature. In this way, we see that even messages that are consciously encoded to convey certain loving feelings and fantasies may nonetheless contain within them deeper unconscious meanings. In most emotional situations, messages are indeed multi-leveled.

MORSE CODE

The word *dot,* denotes a spot, a point, and such; the word *dah* is essentially meaningless. However, the combination of *dot, dot, dot; dah, dah, dah; dot, dot, dot* can be recognized by most individuals as a type of surface encoding that has a formal name: the Morse code. This particular combination of encoded signs represents the letters S-O-S. And while these three letters at first seem meaningless (what is an *SOS*?), there is a broad agreement that they represent, through deliberate encoding, a signal of distress and a call for help. There are, of course, many such forms of deliberate encoding in this very narrow sense.

SLANG

Still another example arises when Ned says to Jenny: "I just grabbed some bread from a hip chick." By the standards of verifiable language, the message is either crude or unintelligible. Why would a man take bread away from a chicken, and is a hip chick one that has huge thighs?

As most of us know, Ned's statement is another form of surface encoding. Developed through a social process and a mixture of conscious and unconscious transformations, it involves a kind of folklore or culturally accepted language that contains generally agreed upon special meanings. The message has been knowingly encoded as a way of stating that Ned had borrowed some money (bread) from a knowledgeable (hip) young woman (chick). According to Ned, she was also a cool cat. Of course, this refers not to a cold feline, but to an understanding, in-tune woman.

There are many forms of this type of automatic conscious encoding, in which the transformations take place entirely on the surface. A single discrete representation here does *not* refer to both itself and to a hidden or latent meaning. These are not forms of double-meaning communications, though they may be so used. They are surface transmissions in which words are used in shared idiosyncratic fashion. The hidden message is evident on the surface as long as one knows the decoding key. All of these are forms of what may be called *horizontal encoding* to indicate that the encoding takes place on the surface and does not penetrate below.

CONSCIOUS VERTICAL ENCODING

While conscious horizontal encoding is usually a matter of convention, a means of establishing a special kind of intimacy, and only rarely used at moments of stress, conscious vertical encoding serves in situations that call for innuendo and indirection. Conscious vertical encoding is, in the main, utilized in situations where direct messages seem inadequate and yet where the emotional pressures have not driven the sender into a state of automatic unconscious encoding. While it is certainly possible for a consciously encoded message to have a third level of meaning that has not been deliberately created by the sender, the main function of this type of message is to soften a blow, to express a need or desire through indirection, and to take advantage of all those situations where something is better half-said.

WOOING BY INDIRECTION

The key to conscious vertical encoding is to select communicative units that have surface logic and meaning but also convey a second, known implication. For example, Fred is in love with Greta. Sitting alone in the corner of a restaurant, he takes her hand and begins to talk. The raw message that quite consciously concerns him the most is that he wants to go to bed with her. Unconsciously, he decides to avoid a frontal approach. The art of seduction (as it is so cruelly and badly named) could not exist without vertically encoded messages. There are, of course, strong individual differences in the capacity to engage successfully and creatively in this type of encoding. Some disguises have the subtlety of a ten-ton truck, others the beauty of a sunset into the Pacific.

As for Fred, he first talks of himself as a sensitive person, incapable of hurting another human being, as gentle and tender. Here the encoding is rather distant from the raw message, which is still difficult to detect. Instead, Fred sends the encoded and heavily disguised plea to understand that were they to have intercourse, Fred would be a sensitive lover.

THE DERIVATIVE MESSAGE ─────────────

Freud (1915) adopted the term *derivative* for a surface message which is derived from and expresses in encoded and defended fashion an underlying (repressed) *raw message*. (For Freud, the raw message was in essence, an unconscious fantasy.) Surface messages tend to vary in the extent to which they convey and express underlying threatening and dangerous raw messages. They range from derivative expressions that are highly meaningful (good carriers of latent meaning) to those that are relatively empty of encoded meaning. Further, under certain conditions, such as the free associations of psychotherapy or in dreams, manifest images are more likely to function as meaningful derivatives than under other conditions, such as a job or some other reality-oriented task, in which it is likely that the sender will utilize relatively non-derivative (single-meaning) surface expressions.

In essence, then, a derivative is an encoded message. A *close derivative* is a surface message with minimal distortion and defense; it is usually rather easily detected and decoded. In contrast, a *distant derivative* is heavily encoded, difficult to unravel, and makes the raw message hard to discern. Fred's initial remark to Greta is a distant derivative. A closer derivative might have been Fred's asking Greta, "What's your attitude about sex?"

Fred next tells Greta that for him, understanding and emotional closeness are important but that physical closeness is the richest and most meaningful form of human intimacy. Here Fred uses a somewhat poetic derivative (encoded messages are beautiful or blunt, imaginative or crude), one that is considerably closer to the raw message. Instead of mentioning intercourse, Fred has said, "physical intimacy," and the rest of the message has been designed to motivate Greta toward a sexual relationship with Fred.

Notice, too, that much of her response would depend on Greta's own state: If she felt defensive and averse to having sexual relations with Fred, she might miss the message entirely; she would probably not engage in any effort at conscious decoding. She might, however, register the encoded meaning unconsciously and respond through a derivative message of her own. On the other hand, if she were in a receptive mood, she would likely consciously decode Fred's message and quickly grasp his intentions. She might even appreciate his imaginative way of expressing himself and his tactfulness. Individuals differ here too, in that some women would no doubt find this kind of indirection cowardly or unmanly.

Finally, Fred tells Greta about his dream. He was in a hammock with a beautiful woman, swinging to and fro in a delightful rhythm. The woman was absolutely enchanting and looked a lot like Greta. Here, of course, the message is even more thinly disguised, a relatively close conscious derivative of the underlying message. Fred takes advantage of a particular message form, the dream, to more boldly convey the underlying raw message he wishes to express. Dreams have an air of innocence, but they are also a way of sending a loaded multi-layered message.

SALES ARE DOWN

Not all is love and seduction in conscious vertical encoding. For example, consider this exchange:

BERT: Sales are down. You've got to do something to cut costs.

CARL: I've got the best cost:price ratio in the district.

BERT: I for one am ready to take a personal salary cut. Things are really that bad.

CARL: Yes, I know. I've done everything I can to economize. Why do you think I didn't hire anyone to replace Arthur? I'm holding down two jobs these days.

Here we see a fascinating interplay between the levels of a sender's and a receiver's modes of expression. One person may be direct while the other encodes; both may be direct and even blunt; both may unconsciously disguise; or both may consciously encode (which is the situation for Carl and Bert).

In examining a message sequence, it is best always to begin with the surface, the manifest content. One must play the game, so to speak, and address the surface even as one plumbs the depths. Quickness of thought and capacity for deliberate encoding are important, but people convey a sense of absurdity and even madness when they address the depths of a message without paying due attention to the direct communication.

The dialogue above begins with the statement of a problem ("Sales are down.")—its manifest stimulus or trigger. Bert directly recommends a particular solution ("cut costs"), and Carl responds defensively, citing evidence that he has economized. Bert then indicates the particular sacrifice he is prepared to make and emphasizes the gravity of the situation. Carl is in full agreement and cites more evidence of his contribution. The entire sequence appears sensible, constructive, and full of meaningful surface exchanges. Why suggest, then, the presence of encoded communication?

The complexities of the dialogue's context prove enormous. In respect to deliberate encoding, it is necessary to be informed about the subjective state of the sender. If a receiver believes he or she has detected an encoded message (and we will confine ourselves for the moment to conscious perception and the direct recognition of meaning), how can he or she be sure that this message was intended by the sender? The problem of verifying the meaning of a manifest message can be difficult.

For example, even so straightforward a statement as "Sales are down" can imply that the company is on the verge of bankruptcy or that Carl is being blamed for the plight of the business. Knowing the *context* for the message would let us limit the possibilities, but this particular manifest message still can *mean* many things. In actuality, Bert was using this comment to develop and disguise a raw message, namely, that he wanted Carl to take a salary cut.

As had Fred in the previous illustration, Bert began his conscious encoding with an implication somewhat distant from his ultimate goal. His compromise is evident: the decrease in salary was communicated through the allusion to the downturn of sales, while the need for defense (avoidance) was satisfied through displacement—it is not Carl's salary that is about to fall, but sales which have already done so.

The suggestion to Carl that he must cut costs is a closer, blunter derivative than, for example, any of the communications from Fred to Greta. The aggression in the raw message has certainly influenced this piece of encoding.

Sensitized by his knowledge of the trigger for these messages (the dire financial problems of the business), Carl was quick to suspect (consciously decode) Bert's underlying but encoded raw message. This realization helped to shape his response in a way that simultaneously offered a direct reaction to Bert's comment and an encoded response to Bert's own encoded message. In commenting, "I've done everything I can to economize," Carl has deliberately encoded his resistance to the unmentioned salary cut.

RESPONDING TO ENCODED MESSAGES

When we receive a deliberately encoded message, we have several choices. First, we can avoid the underlying raw message and pretend it doesn't exist—in which case our responses are likely to be awkward and insensitive to the disguised (latent) issues. This choice is usually a deliberate attempt to frustrate the sender of the encoded communication and attack his or her intended meanings and to simultaneously preclude more meaningful efforts at coping and responsiveness. Had Carl decided to ignore those implications of Bert's two messages which had registered in him consciously, he would have adopted such a course. His responsive messages might have emphasized some detailed plans on how to improve sales or have involved a lecture on methods of cost cutting without mention of salary cutting. A receiver may consciously or unconsciously sense a hidden message, and for reasons of defense or provocation find a clear means to avoid acknowledging the disguised communication. A second choice involves blurting out the encoded raw message as an invitation to deal openly with the underlying issues. Carl could quickly have said to Bert, "Look, if you're leading up to a salary cut, I really don't feel it's justified." The bluntness and even tactlessness of this type of response make it relatively rare. Usually we accept the consciously encoded communication and let the underlying raw meanings emerge gradually, if at all.

The third, and most common, choice is the one that Carl made. Faster than a computer, Carl consciously detects Bert's hidden meaning and quickly composes his own encoded response. His raw reaction is: "I've done all I can to economize; I'll not accept a salary cut." But to state this directly would be rude and provocative.

Bert, quite aware of his own hidden agenda, can quickly read Carl's disguised meaning. Impatient, annoyed, under pressure to get to the issue (his need for expression), and yet not wanting to be blunt (his need for defense), he alludes to his own salary cut. This is, of course, a close-derivative message. It is also extremely common, especially when it comes to unconscious encoding, to encode a message about someone else (especially a threatening perception about that person) in a manifest message about the sender himself or herself (the selective use of displacement). In a dialogue, the safest place to hide a threatening perception of the other person is certainly in a reference to oneself. Many psychoanalysts have been completely fooled by their patient's use of this type of encoding (i.e., by comments patients make about themselves which contain disguised but valid perceptions of their therapists). Here, Bert makes good conscious use of this mechanism by using himself to encode a message meant to allude to Carl—the deliberate use of displacement.

REPRESENTABILITY

Bert's messages foster the study of *representability*. Certain images, those we have termed close derivatives, tend to portray clearly the underlying, raw message. Other images do so poorly; the deeper image is difficult to decipher from the surface expression.

Representability describes degree of portrayal. Realists will represent their view of reality directly, as in a manifest message with only one intended meaning. A more abstract painter compromises, faithful to reality on the one hand, while on the other, portraying it differently from how it actually is. The greater the degree of compromise and distortion, the less direct and immediate the representation. It is even possible to so fragment a particular scene that it becomes totally unrecognizable to the observer. In art, the effect can be brilliant and beautiful; in a communicative relationship, such poor representability destroys meaning and alienates people.

"Sales are down" is a relatively poor representation of the raw message, "I want you to take a salary cut." "You've got to cut costs" represents the raw image even better. "I for one am ready to take a personal salary cut" is more representative still.

THE USE OF COMMUNICATION VERSUS MEANING

In principle, before we explore the underlying meanings of an encoded message, we examine how well these meanings have been represented. Thus the *communicative issue* is to be separated from the problem of meaning. (The communicative issue is of considerable importance but tends to be lost sight of by psychoanalysts interested in meaning. Communicative issues and decisions actually take precedence over those which are dynamic, although the two tend to be dealt with simultaneously in most instances.)

Our ability to communicate with each other depends in large measure on the degree to which we represent directly (manifestly) or indirectly (latently) our raw messages. The more intense the defense, the weaker the representation.

In the dialogue above, Carl, now certain of Bert's underlying raw message, responds to Bert's close derivative with a close derivative of his own. Still avoiding direct mention of his salary cut, Carl offers an encoded defense. Saying that he holds two jobs clearly implies that a salary cut would be unjust. In general, as the consciously encoded messages from one sender grow less and less disguised (and thereby more representational), the messages of the other sender will shift in similar fashion.

TRIGGERS AND CONTEXT

Conscious and unconscious encoding share many features. Therefore we do well to familiarize ourselves with two additional dimensions of deliberate vertical encoding. First let us turn to the role of triggers and contexts.

The decision of whether to encode is made in response to a stimulus or trigger. A stimulus evokes efforts at coping. Although stimuli may on occasion be gratifying, they are often threatening. Were they not, we would need only direct messages. Such dangerous stimuli involve what we may term *raw* (anxiety-provoking) *perceptions* of others and *raw inner fantasies—raw images* in need of automatic (unconscious) or deliberate (conscious) encoding. Thus, the particular situation that triggers encoded messages forms a critical part of the context of communication. Because of this, the trigger and its implications often serve as the best key for decoding multi-leveled communications. We can say that the trigger is the foreground, the immediate stimulus for an encoded message, while the balance of the context is its background and more general setting.

Encoded and direct messages bear the imprint of their stimuli. Bert's comment, "Sales are down," was triggered by a threatening idea like "I must ask Carl to take a salary cut; he's going to raise hell." The trigger, here the raw message, clearly shapes the encoding effort.

Similarly, the trigger for Carl is the realization that even though it was not directly stated, Bert was going to ask him to accept a reduction in salary. This threatening, conscious perception prompted him to emphasize his economizing and his responsibility for two jobs. Clearly, only when we have understood the trigger can we analyze the most compelling and pertinent meanings of surface messages.

THE MECHANISMS OF CONSCIOUS ENCODING ———————

The unconscious encoding of a raw message involves transformations which are carried out, as we saw, mainly through the primary-process mechanisms of condensation, displacement, symbolization, and concern for representability. We also automatically use these very mechanisms in deliberate encoding. It appears that we can in some mysterious way invoke the primary processes at the very same time that we are using, in the main, secondary-process thought.

ENCODING MECHANISMS WORK TOGETHER ———————

Surface encoding tends to be more mundane and less imaginative than unconscious encoding. Still, Carl might have said to Bert, "Look, don't come down so hard on me. Everyone's been giving me a hard time. Some guy came along last night and gouged a huge hole in the side of our house as if he were going to rob us. By some miracle, someone scared him away."

While still encoded, this is a richer message. It respects the need for representability (and is a continuation of the surface dialogue), but it also makes strong use of a number of symbolic images to supplement the efforts at displacement (from the business situation to Carl's home) and condensation (several messages are contained in the single surface expression). In the main, Carl is letting Bert know through a disguised and symbolic expression that he experiences his boss as trying to rob him and, more particularly, as trying to gouge out his insides—to enter his body in order to steal its contents. Carl used this message as a deliberate way of letting his boss know how he was experiencing the unfolding request for him to take a salary cut. We have here the use of a bodily symbol to represent, first, the physical way in which Carl was experiencing the assault on his salary (part of this was, indeed, quite unconscious), and second, to represent as well some of the more hostile and unfair qualities of Bert's messages. In this way, too, Carl is representing his conscious (and to some extent unconscious) perceptions of the trigger which has created the adaptive needs that are satisfied by his own deliberately encoded communications.

The means by which a raw message is encoded work in synchronization. Shifting from one context to another (from direct allusion to indirect expression), from one scene to another, or from one individual to another, is the vital means by which we create a more neutral arena for working through the disturbing triggers that set off the production of encoded expressions. Displacement is therefore one of our most fundamental defenses. Once it has been invoked, we are relatively free to work through (quite unconsciously) extremely difficult issues with considerable abandon.

Often we use little symbolization to supplement this key defense. Thus Carl might suddenly sit back and say, "You know, I've been furious with Mike [another supervisor at the plant]. At times he's so provocative, I could punch him in the nose." The deliberately encoded raw message would be: "You [Bert] are being so provocative, I could punch you in the nose." Carl would have produced a simple example of displacement. If the raw message instead had been, "I could kick you in the genitals," we would then say that in addition to displacement, Carl has used the nose to represent the phallus and the face to portray the genital area. The message would contain displacement from Bert onto Mike as well as upward from Bert's genitals to his face.

Strangely, even conscious vertical encoding operates quite automatically and outside of awareness. You can be sure that Carl did not pause to ask himself whether he were furious with Bert, whether he would like to kick him in the groin, or how he could go about communicating all of these feelings in a way that both expressed his wishes and sufficiently concealed them. Although something like this process did take place, it occurred quite rapidly (during an active, ongoing dialogue) and only occasionally intruded into Carl's conscious awareness.

We can see that symbols can be deliberately used for encoding, depending on the general knowledge and imagination of the sender. Metaphor also lends itself to conscious encoding, although often it has an unconscious element as well. If Carl had said, "Look, I'm not a garbage dump," he would have made use of a metaphor (garbage dump) as a way of encoding his perception of Bert's misuse of him—among other possible meanings.

Prepared by our study of deliberate encoding, let us now move on to unconscious encoding.

CHAPTER 6

UNCONSCIOUS ENCODING: AN INTRODUCTION

We have already identified the basic mechanisms which operate in unconscious encoding. They are the primary-process mechanisms first described by Freud and include condensation, displacement, symbolization, secondary revision, and concerns for representability (i.e., that a meaningful surface message serve as the container for the sometimes disjointed encoded message). The type of secondary-process thinking we use in our daily lives, with its qualities of logic, reality attunement, and the use of discrete elements with single meanings, is totally unsuited for the encoding process. While admirably designed, then, for conscious coping and for situations in which compromise would actually be a disadvantage, it cannot serve under conditions where the avoidance of direct awareness and the use of indirection are vital.

Perhaps the most confusing aspect of decoding is that a perfectly sensible message, one that appears to be the product of secondary-process thinking, has nonetheless been shaped by primary-process mechanisms. The two modes of thinking can work together quite smoothly. To identify those seemingly logical messages that are also products of primary processes we must know the messages' contexts and triggers. The critical determinant is the *functional capacity* of a given message as a response to a specific trigger, rather than any inherent or fixed attribute. A particular communication is certainly chosen unconsciously for what it can express; however, it can express a number of different things.

A WOMAN IS SAWED IN HALF

To illustrate, here is an isolated message:

ANNE: There is a magician doing tricks. He saws a woman in half and then puts her back together into one piece.

This particularly evocative message may suggest a variety of possible meanings. Some messages are relatively flat and barren. For example, "Ship those books to Chicago" is relatively straightforward. Although it might, upon analysis, turn out that the books were used as a symbol for knowledge or for a phallus these considerations seem somewhat forced. Thus although virtually any message may have many meanings, some are far better suited to it than others.

What then of Anne's message? Different triggers and contexts will provide it with distinct encoded meanings. The following are some of the possibilities.

A MAGIC SHOW

Suppose the trigger is a magic show that Anne had attended. She is remembering an illusion she had seen or is telling someone else about it. In this instance, the message is secondary-process dominated: it realistically and logically reports the previous experience. Although one might wonder if the message contains additional encoded meanings, these are superfluous. The main goal of the message is to describe a performance that Anne had seen; the message accomplishes this goal quite well, and Anne moves on to describe other details.

If a receiver proposes that there is also an encoded message in what Anne has said, it too must be seen as secondary. Further, it may or may not have a resemblance to a particular deeply unconscious implication Anne had intended to convey. If indeed Anne was simply listing the details of a recent performance she had witnessed, there would be little reason to believe that this particular message had a special hidden meaning. If, on the other hand, she had selected this allusion for concentrated comment or shown other signs of intense concern with its implications, we might readily suspect that it had special meaning for Anne and that by discussing it she was trying to work through an underlying issue. But in the context described, Anne's message is primarily logical, realistic, with a single meaning.

BOY KILLS GIRL

Suppose instead this message describes a dream or some of Anne's conscious musings. Suppose she had been musing about an incident with her boyfriend and had then recalled this particular part of a magic performance she had seen some days earlier. That recollection *might* fit logically into a sequence about her social relationship, but there is a strong likelihood that it occurred to Anne because it suited her emotional and communicative needs in some deeply important way.

Anne had been thinking of a fight she had had with her boyfriend, Harry, the previous evening. He had lost control during intercourse and had become physically and verbally abusive. She was experiencing considerable anger as she recalled the incident. The image of the performance had intruded into her train of thought, although it seemed to her logically connected in that she had seen the show with Harry. Nonetheless, unexpected and intrusive thoughts of this kind often contain important encoded communications.

In brief, Anne was dealing with a raw, unconscious perception of her boyfriend to the effect that he had some need to be overwhelmingly powerful and that he intended to assault and destroy her. While conscious of the hurtful qualities of his behavior, Anne was not aware that she had perceived him as wanting to murder her. Such a perception was terrifying and intensified her conflict, because she also had strong loving feelings for Harry.

The raw message that required automatic encoding was the perception that her boyfriend wished to murder Anne. Anne needed to experience its impact and to adapt to it, and yet she could not do so directly without risking panic. As a result, she disguised the perception.

First she used the disguise *displacement.* Instead of thinking of the scene in the bedroom with Harry, Anne recalls a scene at a theater in the presence of the same man. Not only does the setting change, but also the central figure—from Harry to the magician. Once again, displacement appears at the heart of the expression of a multiple message. In fact, displacement creates at least two messages: that which pertains to the original raw image, and that which pertains to the replacement, displaced image. In a sense, then, displacement implies *condensation,* although we usually use that term when several different raw images combine into a single, manifest element. (In order to identify the operation of condensation, it is necessary to know several triggers for a single message or several different sets of associations which flow from a particular surface element. We will therefore touch upon the use of condensation later on.)

Anne quite effectively uses *symbolism*. She represents a raw perception—fantasies of an attempt at murder and a wish to tear apart her vagina—with the muted image of a magician sawing a woman in half. In this way, she *represents* or portrays the violence she believed was being done to her, while modifying its assaultive qualities.

If, instead, Anne had dreamt of a woman being cut in half by a train, the use of symbolism or substitute representation would have failed her. The horror and violence of the raw image would not have been modified, and there would have been little sense of a successful defensive operation. The manifest image Anne unconsciously chose presents an act of violence that is not an act of violence, an image of being cut in half that is not being cut in half. It would be hard to imagine a more successful defense and compromise in that the violence is represented in a manner that is immediately reassuring and a grim reality made into a pleasant unreality. The defense is reinforced by the final image in which the woman is once again whole.

Secondary revision and *concerns for representability* show their influence in the selection of this particular surface image in that the memory is part of a chain of thoughts regarding Harry. Unconsciously, we are always searching for dreams, memories, daily events, and other ways to express our logical train of thought and simultaneously to encode raw messages in need of disguise.

GIRL CASTRATES BOY

The same stimulus for Anne's image (the incident with Harry), creates another message. Through *condensation*, Anne encodes another raw message, namely, her wish to castrate Harry. Thus the surface image of the magician sawing the woman in half, through displacement and symbolization, portrays Anne's fantasy of cutting off Harry's penis. Anne did not think consciously that she would like to castrate her lover. Consciously, she felt angry and vengeful, with only some fleeting thoughts about not seeing him again. Thus, this particular raw message (wishful fantasy) never did reach consciousness; only its encoded expression did so. Here again the compromise between the need to be aware and the need for defense is self-evident.

Now that we know that there were two raw messages, one a perception and the other a fantasy, combined in the single manifest image, we can appreciate the role of condensation. This mechanism serves mental economy; it lets us take care of several problems at one time. In life, the presence of several emotional problems at a given moment is extremely common. Condensation spares the individual the necessity of an endless stream of encoded adaptive messages by combining several such communications into a single manifest expression. Of course, secondary revision and concern for representability are also at work in condensed messages.

A PARENT DIES

As a final means of demonstrating that this same manifest message could contain a dramatically different raw message, let us suppose that its trigger had been the death of Anne's mother. Consciously, Anne feels considerable grief and misses her mother, with whom she was quite close. She thinks vaguely that the doctor who had operated on her mother for abdominal cancer might have saved her life. But Anne understands this as an unrealistic wish. By the time of the surgery, Anne's mother's cancer was terminal.

Inevitably, on the death of a beloved person, many conflicting emotions and disturbing raw fantasies and perceptions arise. Anne, for example, perceived the surgeon as assaultive, as cutting her mother in half. She was unaware of this perception, since consciously she understood the nature of the surgery and saw it as a necessary medical procedure. Nonetheless, through *displacement* (from the surgeon to the magician) and *symbolization* (the surgery is symbolized by the sawing), Anne had produced an unconsciously encoded message.

Anne also had a terribly painful wish that her mother were still alive. While this wish was at times conscious, it also obtained encoded expression in this particular memory. There, the woman is put back in one piece, magically and miraculously restored to good health. Anne deeply wished on one level that such miracles could really take place. She did not tolerate such attitudes in herself and found them unbearably conflictual and painful; as a result, she resorted to a more comfortable encoded version of these fantasy-wishes. Here, too, *displacement* and *symbolization* were in operation. Through *condensation* both the image of the surgeon and the painful wish that her mother were still alive found simultaneous expression.

We can see now that it is indeed quite possible for a single manifest image to be used unconsciously to encode a wide range of raw, unconscious fantasies and perceptions, each with a rather different meaning.

CHAPTER 7

UNCONSCIOUS ENCODING: ORIGINS WITH FREUD

DREAM WORK AND DREAM THOUGHT

We owe our understanding of unconscious encoding to Sigmund Freud who, in *The Interpretation of Dreams*, eloquently detailed and documented the means by which the raw messages which underlie our dreams (*dream thoughts,* as he termed them) are shaped into a manifest dream experience. The operations involved are the primary-process mechanisms, and Freud termed such efforts the *dream work*. Freud showed that there are three basic components to a dream (and to all encoded messages): (1) the latent dream thought (the raw message); (2) the manifest dream (the encoded communication); and (3) the dream work (the mechanisms which transform the latent into the manifest dream).

DAY RESIDUE

For Freud, virtually every dream thought that requires transformation and working through in a dream is prompted by events on the day of the dream. While many of these day residues seem quite innocuous, Freud demonstrated that they consistently connect to underlying issues of considerable emotional importance. Freud was implying that the day residues for dreams are themselves encoded messages. He showed that these stimuli had emotional meaning not only in the present, but also touched on important early experiences. In sum, the encoded message of a dream is stimulated by a daytime experience with its own conscious and unconscious meanings.

Freud proposed that dreams are the fulfillment of wishes, present and past (adult and infantile). Although Freud placed the unconscious wish at the heart of the dream, he demonstrated quite clearly that dreams were night-time efforts designed to work over, work through, and adapt to ongoing conflicts and emotional problems.

FREUD'S SELF-ANALYSIS

Freud became concerned with dreams quite early in his career as a psychiatrist; he studied their manifestations in his patients in the 1880s and especially in the 1890s. Many of his early insights into the nature of dreams, however, came from the investigation of his own dreams. This work formed the substance of *The Interpretation of Dreams* (1900). We will therefore turn now to two of Freud's dreams, discussed in that volume, as a means of illustrating both unconscious encoding and trigger (day residue) decoding.

THE WISH TO SUCCEED

In Chapter 4 of the dream book, Freud reports the following dream (pp. 137–141);

I. My friend R. was my uncle—I had a great feeling of affection for him.

II. I saw before me his face, somewhat changed. It was as though it had been drawn out lengthways. A yellow beard that surrounded it stood out especially clearly.

In most of Freud's dream analyses, he provided a preamble that described the circumstances surrounding the dream and then reported some of his associations to the specific elements of the manifest dream. In this way he arrived at (he decoded) the latent dream thoughts. Once he had defined these latent images, he could identify how the transformation from latent to manifest expression had taken place.

In the dream quoted above, the context involved Freud's concerns about being recommended for an appointment as "*professor extraordinarous*" at the university. Freud had little hope that he would get the position. At the time, a colleague who had also been recommended (though not appointed) reported to Freud that someone at the Offices of Ministry had told him that the delay involved "denominational considerations" of the kind that also applied to Freud. It was this event that had served as the day residue and had prompted the dream that same night.

Freud's main associations refer to a particular uncle, Josef, who had gotten involved in illegal financial transactions for which he was punished. He was thought of as a simpleton. The face in the dream neatly combined the visages of this Uncle Josef with Freud's friend R. (note the use of condensation).

Another line of associations involved a different colleague, N., who had also been recommended for a professorship. He had not received the appointment and had met Freud a few days earlier, indicating that a factor in his fate might well have been a case a woman patient had brought against him. The case had been dismissed, but it had left his reputation blemished. Thus (again through the process of condensation), the image in the dream (of Freud's Uncle Josef) represented Freud's uncle himself and Freud's two colleagues who had not been appointed to professorships. Through Freud's associations to his uncle, one of these colleagues was characterized as a simpleton and the other as a criminal.

Freud now saw his underlying dream wish (the latent dream thought or raw message): If both R. and N. had not received their appointments for denominational reasons, Freud's own appointment was also open to doubt. If, on the other hand (and this is the wish expressed in the dream), there were other reasons for their failure, Freud's hopes could remain undimmed.

To this point, then, Freud had encoded several raw images. The dream's central wish (connected to related childhood wishes) finds encoded and considerably disguised expression when Freud dreams that his friend R. is his uncle. Making use of displacement, symbolic representation, and condensation, Freud represents both R. and N. in a manner that implies reasons for their failure to obtain their appointments which would not apply to Freud. Freud was reluctant to register consciously that his colleagues had such failings. Yet driven by his own needs to succeed, Freud's dream encodes his wishes in a seemingly innocuous fashion.

Though Freud does not touch upon the possibility, it may well be that his dream also reflects encoded unconscious *perceptions* of actual traits in his two colleagues, attributes which Freud was loath to recognize openly. Because of his fear of antagonizing his associates and his disturbance over his unpleasant view of them, Freud may well have disguised these perceptions in creating this dream.

Freud also associates to a feeling of affection that he has for R. in the dream. This feeling strikes him as false, ungenuine, and exaggerated and appears to Freud to be a representation of its opposite, the wish to slander R. Freud proposes therefore that his latent dream thought was to harm R. Through a particular form of symbolization frequently used in dreams, turning something into its opposite, Freud had found an apt means of disguising and defending himself against the open expression of this particular impulse.

Through the presentation of a large array of dream analyses of this kind, Freud constructed a detailed understanding of dream mechanisms and meanings that still serve us well. The five characteristics of primary-process thinking which he postulated have stood the test of time. However it has been possible to demonstrate that symbolic representation includes such defense mechanisms as reversal or turning into the opposite, isolation (creating a distance between connected elements), and projection (attributing aspects of oneself to someone else)—among others.

THE RELUCTANT HOSTESS

Another brief dream (of a patient) reported by Freud (p. 147) follows:

I wanted to give a supper-party, but I had nothing in the house but a little smoked salmon. I thought I would go out and buy something, but remembered then that it was Sunday afternoon and all the shops would be shut. Next I tried to ring up some caterers, but the telephone was out of order. So I had to abandon my wish to give a supper-party.

Freud was struck with how this dream seemed on the surface to be both sensible and coherent and in addition did not seem to express the fulfillment of a wish. Thus this was either a dream that reflected secondary-process mechanisms or one that resulted from the operation of both primary- and secondary-process thinking. As Freud knew, however, this issue could be resolved only with an analysis of the dream based on the patient's associations.

The patient associated to her husband's wish to lose weight and his comment to a portrait painter that the painter would no doubt prefer a piece of a pretty young girl's behind to the whole of his (the husband's) face. The patient had also begged her husband to not give her any caviar so that she could go on teasing him about his not doing so.

Freud felt that these associations were defensive and that they did not illuminate the latent dream thoughts. He pressed the patient further. She finally recalled being with a woman friend whom her husband constantly praised. The friend was quite thin, and the patient's husband praised her despite his usual admiration for a plumper figure. The friend had then asked the patient to invite her to dinner since the patient fed her guests so well.

Notice how, in associating to the dream, this patient initially had avoided its most meaningful day residue or stimulus. The visit with the friend had taken place on the day of the dream, and once it had been revealed, the latent dream thoughts emerged. Freud showed his patient that the dream expressed her wish to not have a supper-party in order to not feed her woman friend, who would use it to get stout and attract her husband still more. The dream was therefore the fulfillment of a wish and the transformation of a disturbing mixture of latent perception and fantasy. The patient wanted to give nothing to her friend. She may also have perceived unconsciously a greater attraction between her husband and her friend than she had perceived consciously. These disturbing perceptions were encoded into a well-disguised dream of not giving the supper-party. Here, too, the main mechanisms appear to involve displacement, a large measure of symbolization, and secondary revision. Condensation was also at work in that the patient wanted neither her husband nor her friend to gratify themselves at her (the patient's) expense.

There is evidence here too of the way in which *repression*, another basic mental mechanism, contributes to dream formation. Repression is subsumed under the category of symbolism (which, as we noted, may be thought of in a broad sense to include not only the specific use of symbolic substitute representations, but also to include all factors that change raw dream images into manifest dream elements). Through repression, a fantasy is cut off from access to consciousness and in some sense forgotten. We know of its existence because it presses for expression and does so in compromised fashion.

In this dream, the patient represses all her images of her husband and friend and dreams only about the supper-party and her own frustrated efforts to arrange it. The underlying conflicts are so repressed that when the patient began to associate to the dream, she made no connection whatsoever to her friend. We may assume that Freud's pressure on the patient broke down her defenses and resistance and permitted some measure of disguised expression of the underlying, repressed material.

Freud wanted confirmation of his solution of the dream. He therefore asked about the smoked salmon, and the patient recalled that it was her friend's favorite dish. Freud thus got evidence from an entirely different route that the dream did indeed involve raw messages (images of fantasy and perception) related to the friend.

Finally, Freud offered a related but different interpretation of this dream. He suggested that the patient actually was a stand-in for her friend and that the frustration of the patient's wishes in the dream served through displacement and symbolization as an expression of the patient's wish that her friend's needs not be fulfilled. Freud stressed the fact that dreams are multi-layered and contain, as a rule, several levels of meaning. Each dream affords several interpretations because each dream conveys through condensation several major messages.

In both of the dreams Freud analyzed, the secret message contained in the dream became clear with the identification of its trigger or day residue. This fact lends support to the thesis that unconscious encoding is an automatic and adaptive response to disturbing stimuli. At the time that Freud discovered the secrets of the dream, there was virtually no meaningful theory of the basis for emotional illness and only a confusing smattering of writings on dreams. Throughout his life, Freud considered *The Interpretation of Dreams* one of the most important volumes he ever wrote. There is no doubt that it was the work of a remarkable genius at the height of his creativity.

CHAPTER 8

UNCONSCIOUS ENCODING IN OUR DAILY LIVES

In general, unconscious encoding is instinctive and, so to speak, takes care of itself. We study it carefully mainly to familiarize ourselves with the means by which encoded messages are created. This provides a useful guide to decoding efforts, which reverse or undo these very processes. In this chapter, we will study an incident in the lives of two individuals in which unconscious encoding played a notable role. It will provide us with a final basis for understanding this special mode of thinking (encoding) and how it operates.

"YOU'VE BEEN ALOOF ALL NIGHT"

Isabel and John were a young married couple. One evening, they watched a play on television. Despite occasional comments from Isabel, John was silent and seemed moody. Toward the end of the evening, the following dialogue occurred:

ISABEL: John, you've been aloof all night. Let's go to bed.

JOHN: Have you seen my pipe?

ISABEL: I'm in the mood. That television show was a turn on. Come to bed with me. There's a full moon out there.

JOHN: In a little while. Where's my damn pipe? I'm also short of tobacco; I never have what I need. Maybe I ought to try a new brand.

ISABEL: You know, I keep thinking of that woman, the one in the story. Her husband was so hurtful to her. And she suffered so much from her miscarriage. Her involvement with that young boy gave her something for the moment, but was it really worth it? She was only hurt more in the long run. But she sure had reason for being unfaithful. What would you have done if you were in her place?

JOHN: I don't know. Maybe her husband needed help. Maybe she should have tried harder with him.

We have here a series of messages that conform to secondary-process mechanisms. They are faithful to reality, direct, logical, and meaningful on the surface. As is true of all communicative exchanges, they involve surface triggers which unfold in sequence, now from one person and then from the other. Thus John's aloofness had triggered Isabel's initial response, while John responded to Isabel's invitation with avoidance. Isabel then tried to entice her husband to bed, while he responded by continuing to put her off. Isabel then shifted to the story in order to comment on it and to ask John a question. He then responded with his opinion.

Although there are some ambiguities in these exchanges, we will not concern ourselves with a further analysis of their surface. There is a sense of evident conflict without a sign of resolution. There is tension, although we have little idea of its basis.

SIGNS OF UNCONSCIOUS ENCODING

In reviewing this dialogue, we can ask whether there are any signs of the possible use of encoded messages. As we know, there need not be, and yet we might discover the presence of unconscious encoding.

To answer, there are indeed certain clues that the encoding process is in operation. For example, there is the sense of unresponsiveness in John. Disconnected exchanges often suggest the presence of encoded communication. Further, the allusion to dreams, our own creative efforts, the creativity of others, rich images, and complex but meaningful narratives are also excellent carriers of encoded messages; their presence suggests the likelihood of primary-process influence. In all, the absence of accumulated meaning in a set of sequential messages from a single person, the presence of responses which seem relatively unrelated to their immediate triggers, and the use of message forms that serve well as the carriers of encoded messages, are among the signs that unconscious encoding may well be in operation.

PRELIMINARY CONSCIOUS ENCODING

In our attempt to recognize the presence of encoding, let us look first for possible forms of *conscious* encoding in this dialogue. "Let's go to bed" is an inferential message, containing a colloquial or socially agreed upon form of surface horizontal encoding: the term is often used to represent sexual intercourse. The same applies to the phrase "turn on," while the allusion to the full moon was a deliberate encoding of a seductive message and sexual longing. In these messages, by and large, the ratio of revelation to concealment is quite high; the former appears to predominate.

In addition, the specific mention of the full moon contained within it a form of conscious encoding that touched upon a shared latent or hidden meaning developed personally between these two marital partners. For some reason quite unknown to her, Isabel tended to be somewhat stiff and distant in bed at most times. However, in the presence of a full moon, she tended to loosen up and be a relaxed and gratifying sexual partner.

In all, then, these selected instances of conscious encoding involve messages that Isabel did not wish to convey directly and which she consciously thought would be more effective in encoded fashion. As a product of creativity, there is indeed a special quality to the deliberately well-chosen (poetic or near-poetic) encoded communication. Faced with John's distance, Isabel almost instinctively felt that the indirect approach would be more effective and that a direct effort at seduction might only antagonize her husband.

THE DIALOGUE'S UNCONSCIOUS ENCODING: ISABEL

With all this in mind, we will turn now to the subject of unconscious encoding. The broad context for this sequence actually involved a dispute between Isabel and John. Isabel wanted to get pregnant, but John was reluctant to have a child. He preferred to maintain their freedom as a couple and was also wary of the loss of income from Isabel's job. As a direct result, he had been antagonistic and distant, while Isabel had alternated between being seductive and entreating, and rather nasty and chiding.

THE TRIGGER

The most immediate trigger for this dialogue had been a specific discussion at supper of these problems. Isabel suspected that she was ovulating and wanted to have relations; John maintained a noncommital attitude.

With this situation as the trigger, we are now in a position to identify a series of consciously and unconsciously encoded messages not previously discernible. On the surface, Isabel's allusion to John's aloofness contains in encoded form a criticism of his sexual distance. John's question as to whether Isabel had seen his pipe is a deliberately encoded message designed to imply that he wished to be left alone and was not interested in having intercourse. Isabel then replied in a way designed to convey her excitement; however, an additional meaning can now be ascribed to the deliberately encoded implications of the allusion to the full moon. John had said that he would make his wife pregnant on a night that they could hear a wolf howling to a full moon. Beyond this point, the meanings of the dialogue shade so strongly into unconscious encoding, we will not pursue these deliberately encoded messages any further.

THE FULL MOON

While we will concentrate on the latter part of this dialogue, from here on it is well to begin with Isabel's message about the full moon. As we have seen, this referred simultaneously (through condensation) to a realistic fact, to an encoded message regarding Isabel's sexual availability, and to a promise made by her husband.

Love for John.   In addition, it carried additional meanings of which Isabel was not consciously aware. The first of these was once again highly personal in that it was a symbolic representation of the night in the mountains with John when, under the glow of a full summer moon, she had first shared a sense of love with him. Thus at a moment when Isabel mainly felt resentment toward her husband, and entertained no conscious thoughts or memories to the contrary, she was expressing her deep sense of love for her husband through this particular encoded message. Simultaneously, via condensation the same message turned her anger into its opposite, love, and served a primarily defensive function in light of the trigger of John's refusal to have intercourse with her and to attempt to conceive. This same message not only was unconsciously designed to convey a series of meanings to John, but also was self-directed and part of Isabel's attempt to resolve her direct conflict with John and her inner conflict of mixed feelings toward him.

Love for another man.   Still another message was contained in the allusion to the full moon, this one involving a different memory. A year or so before she had met John, Isabel had been on vacation at the shore. She had met a man named Ben and spent a romantic night on the beach, lying with him under a beautiful full moon. She was strongly attracted to Ben, who had had to leave the next morning, but who promised to see her when they both returned to the city. Their lovemaking that one night was extremely gratifying for Isabel and led to many daydreams of him. While Ben never called her again, in her imagination he soon became the epitome of the virile (and, of late, impregnating) man.

While Isabel had not thought consciously of this incident with Ben, this brief allusion to the full moon served to encode an elaborate unconscious fantasy of being married to and impregnated by this man. Through the use of repression (there is no specific mention of Ben), displacement, symbolization, and great disguise, Isabel was able to express this hidden wish (raw message) in a form that neither she nor her husband recognized. Clearly, its direct expression would have been painful to both, a fact that helps to account for the intensity of this particular unconscious encoding effort.

The primal scene.   Finally, condensed into this single image of a full moon is a childhood memory of a time when Isabel had inadvertently entered her parents' bedroom while they were having intercourse. During the dialogue, she had no direct memory of that particular experience, an event that she had not remembered in some years. At the time of the experience, Isabel had thought that her father was doing some kind of violence to her mother. Thus, contained in the encoded memory itself is either a wish to do violence to John, or a fear that John, in impregnating her, would do violence to her. Then, too, there is the unconscious perception of the destructiveness in John's attitude, as well as Isabel's responsive hostility.

At times of enormous stress, individuals will pack (condense) into a single allusion a series of complicated fantasies, memories, and perceptions, all of which have been subjected to some degree of unconscious encoding. Complex situations call for complex adaptive responses, and intensely encoded communications are among the best means of intrapsychic and interpersonal adaptation. Further, the encoded expressions must either eventually become conscious so they may be directly effective or lead in some fashion to directly adaptive behaviors.

THE TELEVISION PLAY

Another message sequence that contains a series of unconsciously encoded messages from Isabel involve her reference to the television play. Triggered by her husband's rejection and its implications, Isabel had on the surface given up trying to persuade him to go to bed with her. She decided to change the subject and to discuss the play. Without thinking of the possible implications and with a real event that justified her selection, she mentioned certain elements: the hateful, hurtful husband; the woman's miscarriage; the woman's involvement with the young boy. In light of the context and trigger, and with the help of Isabel's associations which will follow, we may identify the encoded messages contained in this communication.

To consider a few highlights, the woman in the story had set off a series of memories that touched upon Isabel's relationship with John. None of these was conscious, and they found expression only at the point when Isabel began to feel a great deal of anger toward her husband and a strong sense of conflict. These feelings motivated her to engage in defensive yet revealing encoded expressions.

John had had a brief affair early in their marriage, a hurtful experience that Isabel thought of from time to time and had even considered in passing while watching the story. Because of the threat involved, the memory had been set to the side, only to find expression in disguised fashion at this point in Isabel's dialogue with her husband.

The woman's extramarital affair. The key surface representation of this particular raw message, a painful memory, is the woman's affair with the young boy. Here, there is displacement, though little in the way of symbolization (merely the change of sexes), secondary revision, and as will be shown soon, condensation.

At the same time, the allusion to the affair contained in encoded form a much deeper, threatening, and therefore more disguised raw image. In response to the trigger of her husband's hurtful indifference, Isabel was here experiencing a heavily encoded unconscious homosexual fantasy through which she herself could be close to (have an affair with) a woman. The affair would give her something. On a deeper level, based on early childhood fantasies, this gift would be impregnation (as a small child, Isabel entertained conscious and later unconscious, encoded fantasies that women could impregnate other women). Here the encoding process has made use of condensation, displacement (from a woman at work whom Isabel found attractive to the woman in the story), symbolization (including reversal and the use of an affair between a woman and a young boy to represent an affair between two women), and secondary revision (the use of the television program).

As we have seen, some raw messages are more threatening than others. In this instance, the aroused homosexual fantasies were far more disturbing than Isabel's hurtful memory of her husband's affair. In part, the degree of disguise and the distance between the manifest image and the latent content are proportional to the degree of threat generated by the underlying raw message. It follows too that less disguised messages are more readily decoded than those that are heavily disguised and that a sender is more likely to acknowledge the meanings of a decoded message of lesser threat than one that would cause him or her greater distress.

Because of the stressful qualities of the situation and Isabel's deep wish to have a child, once her husband became so intensely frustrating, her choice was either a direct attack or a shift to encoded messages. The latter enabled Isabel to experience on some level, however unconsciously, a variety of perceptions of her husband (his hateful qualities, his lack of fidelity, and the way in which she perceived him as pushing her toward an affair with someone else), while simultaneously encoding a number of responsive fantasies and wishes (to have an affair, heterosexual or homosexual; to be hateful and hurt her husband; and, in contrast, *not* to act in these ways at all). Finally, the allusion to the miscarriage condensed Isabel's rage at her husband, her fears that he would be incapable of impregnating her, her worries that she was incapable of conceiving, her wishes to destroy (abort) her marriage, and her feelings about an abortion that her mother had had when Isabel was a child—to name but a few. Through encoded messages, then, Isabel was able to intensely work over a vast array of feelings, fantasies, and perceptions related to her current plight, as well as their echoes in earlier experiences from childhood and adulthood.

THE DIALOGUE'S
UNCONSCIOUS ENCODING: JOHN

There is, of course, much more encoded in this last message of Isabel's. Leaving further speculation to the reader, let us turn instead to John's communications for a brief moment.

THE TRIGGER

Well outside of his awareness, John's search for his pipe was triggered, first, by his wife's wish to have intercourse and to be impregnated, and second, by recent sexual experiences with Isabel during which he had been impotent. Utilizing a well-known symbol, John expressed several underlying raw messages with his seemingly simple question. Most striking are his hope for potency, his perception of his own impotency, and his wish that his wife would be more helpful in enabling him to maintain an erection. Her disappointment and hostility over his earlier failures to impregnate her had contributed to John's sexual difficulties.

It follows, then, that John made use of displacement (from his penis to the pipe), condensation (the expression of multiple underlying raw messages in one surface image), symbolic representation (the pipe for his penis), and secondary elaboration (John had indeed misplaced his favorite pipe and had a realistic need for his wife's help in finding it).

We can readily see too that John encoded his concerns about his potency in his comments about being short of tobacco, never having what he needs, and that he ought to try a new brand. At the same time, this sequence encodes his unconscious perception of his wife as unhelpful and denying him what he requires; it also portrays an unconscious fantasy of being potent with a different woman, a thought that John had not entertained consciously.

Finally, through another encoded message John acknowledges his own need for help, as well as encoding his wife's requirements in this regard. In his final message, he reprimands his wife for not trying harder with him, all of this outside of awareness and through the full use of the primary-process mechanisms.

In actuality, this entire sequence contains dozens of additional unconsciously encoded messages. Remarkably, under certain conditions, an enormous amount of information is exchanged entirely outside of the awareness of all concerned. And yet, without an ability to properly decode the manifest expressions into latent contents, each party to such a dialogue is severely limited in respect to both understanding and coping ability. While unconscious sensitivities are indeed useful, many reactions to other persons prove to be quite inappropriate and maladaptive when they are determined by unrecognized unconscious contents and functions. The best possible adaptation takes place in the presence of well-defined *conscious* knowledge, developed through self-analysis and the understanding of others and the conscious working over of previously unconscious factors. There is considerable difference between conscious mastery and control, and being at the mercy of unrecognized needs, fantasies, and perceptions.

Ultimately, this type of resourcefulness depends on the development of a sound method for decoding messages. Let us therefore turn to this problem at once.

CHAPTER 9

INDICATIONS OF THE PRESENCE OF UNCONSCIOUS ENCODING

The decoding process is designed to reverse or undo the consequences of encoding. Its fulcrum is the identification of the trigger for the message at hand. The trigger itself has to be treated as an encoded message, understood as a response to still another stimulus and in terms of manifest and latent implications. The more we know of the specific and broader contexts of a message and of an individual's private associations to it, the more likely it is that our decoding efforts will be both definitive and successful.

In daily life, we are seldom in a well-structured, standardized, and controlled situation in which these various factors can be carefully evaluated. Not surprisingly, then, the decoding process is usually fraught with difficulties and dangers. With caution and understanding, however, most of these can be overcome.

OVERDECODING AND UNDERDECODING

A critical decision involves whether to treat a particular message in terms of its manifest meanings or its evident latent implications, or both. It is possible to (1) overdecode by ascribing unconscious meanings to a message that was intended consciously and unconsciously by the sender to have little more than manifest implications; or (2) underdecode, and to miss important encoded communications because of the natural tendency to take such matters at face value.

Full and careful decoding requires considerable and deliberate measures by the receiver of a message. People tend toward simplistic listening, surface considerations, and accepting things at face value. (A pathological exception to this trend is seen with those individuals who are distinctly paranoid and attempt to read many meanings into the simplest of communications.) Nonetheless, this propensity is relatively understandable in that only dangerous and threatening messages are encoded, and the decoder immediately takes the risk of a confrontation with painful truths about others (especially the sender) and himself or herself (many messages involve valid unconscious perceptions of the receiver of which he or she is quite unaware) that he or she might well avoid by sticking with manifest contents. It is here that the liabilities of true knowledge can be identified. It poses a threat that may help to account for the general failure in the eighty or so years since the publication of *The Interpretation of Dreams* (Freud 1900) of both therapists and patients to develop a truly valid decoding method (this in essence would involve trigger decoding). Since defensive needs are great, self-invested distortions inevitable, and the possibility of misreadings considerable, all efforts at decoding must be carried out with humility and caution.

In this chapter, we will consider both conscious and unconscious decoding. We have already seen that the decoding of hidden messages may take place automatically and unconsciously, entirely outside of the awareness of the receiver and decoder. Under threatening circumstances, it is typical for us only to register consciously and directly a portion of a communication from someone else; the rest is perceived subliminally or unconsciously. We learn of this tendency in analyzing a receiver's responses. They reveal in their own encoded fashion the unconscious influence of what has been taken in. Thus raw, unconscious perceptions that are automatically subjected to the encoding process are an important dimension of human communication. In our analysis of the triggers for responses, we will place considerable stress on this type of communicative interchange.

Finally, it is well to realize that in most instances, this type of unconscious perception and decoding is quite faithful (true) to the consensually validated meanings of the received messages. While there are indeed instances of erroneous or false unconscious perceptions, most of the processing and understanding that we carry out on an unconscious level is faithful to the manifest and latent meanings of the realities involved.

INDICATORS OF HIDDEN MESSAGES

Ultimately, the determination that a particular message contains an important latent communication involves the full assessment of its triggers. There are, however, actually seven overlapping signs that a particular message is likely to contain hidden meanings and purposes. It is helpful for listeners to be familiar with these indicators. It is highly economical and emotionally stabilizing to know when to listen in terms of single-meaning manifest expressions and when to think seriously of searching for hidden meanings and purposes. Considerable difficulty arises when a heavily encoded message is taken at face value and, similarly, when a single message is assigned a number of unnecessary and fanciful disguised meanings.

We should also remember that the decoding process needs some means of *validation* before we can feel confident of our efforts. There is also considerable distinction between a private and subjective effort at decoding and imparting the results to a sender. As already noted, the creator of a message may or may not be aware of or open to its hidden meanings (after all, it has been necessary for him or her to encode the dangerous raw message in the first place). Because of this, an added measure of caution is required in these endeavors. It is quite offensive to propose an encoded meaning to someone who recognizes only his or her conscious intentions; it requires considerable tact and sensitivity to make use of this kind of understanding, and to apply it convincingly to an unwary sender.

SEVEN SIGNS OF HIDDEN MESSAGES

The seven clues, then, of the presence or likelihood of a hidden message are the following:

DISCORDANCE WITH REALITY

Any message that does not seem entirely realistic, logical, and complete is likely to contain hidden meaning. However, to make this determination, both the trigger and the wider context must be fully understood. Because of the subjective factors involved, an evaluation of this kind is quite risky and open to personal bias and error. As with all such formulations, efforts should be made to validate with evidence from other sources the impression that an important encoded message is being conveyed.

To illustrate, suppose a boss, Ken, invites an employee, Larry, into his office. Within a few minutes, Ken has told Larry that he is fired. Larry then asks why. The boss offers an explanation, and Larry attempts to defend his position and to offer sensible reasons why he should not be let go. In this type of message exchange, there is little suggestion of encoded meaning, and the surface of the dialogue seems to account for almost all of its implications.

Suppose, however, that Larry had stared at his boss with puzzlement and then said, "You know, the way you look now makes me think of a picture of a man in today's newspaper. There is really a strong resemblance. He murdered his boyfriend; they were homosexuals. He will probably get the electric chair."

In the second instance, Larry's response does not seem clearly related to the trigger for his message, and it does not fit well, on the surface, with the overall situation. There is a sense of illogic and confusion, of a break in relatedness between the messages from Ken and from Larry. Such signs of discordance and inappropriateness suggest the presence of a heavily encoded message.

It appears that Larry is under a strong compulsion to express and defend against an unconscious perception of his boss as a killer, and of his own wish to murder his boss in turn. The allusion to homosexuality touches upon unconsciously perceived (and never at all conscious) indications of a latent homosexual and seductive set of feelings in Ken toward Larry, and in Larry toward Ken. It appears that Larry is unconsciously (via an encoded expression) suggesting to Ken that a critical source of the decision to fire him involves these unconscious homosexual conflicts. Clearly, these are all powerful raw messages, many of which Larry was entirely unaware of; they required automatic and unconscious encoding in order to be communicated in disguised (displaced) form.

Larry's messages left Ken with a sense of puzzlement and uncertainty. Why in the world, he wondered, was Larry talking like this and not reacting directly to being fired? This type of experience is typical in those situations where one individual is communicating largely on a manifest level, while the other is expressing himself or herself through encoded messages. Meaningful communicative exchanges usually require that both parties to a dialogue operate mainly through the same mode of expression; however, when both are functioning in terms of primary-process mechanisms, there is a strong likelihood of confusion and misunderstanding.

Finally, notice too how important it is for Ken to recognize the presence of an encoded communication from Larry, and to engage in some effort at decoding the meanings of the latter's messages. Were he to do so successfully, he would then be able to respond sensitively to the violence involved, and, if he were at all sophisticated and insightful, to the messages regarding the underlying homosexuality. These are indeed extremely burdensome messages to deal with. Nonetheless, failing to appreciate these implications could make it quite difficult for Ken to deal with Larry at this time.

CONTRADICTORY MESSAGES

In examining a series of messages from a single sender, we may discover that one or more elements in the sequence do not appear to fit well with the rest. Because of the power of the trigger, a group of message units tend to develop their meanings around one or two central themes. As long as each message unit contributes manifestly to the development of those themes, and there is no other sign of unconscious encoding, there is little reason to suspect the presence of a hidden message. It is the appearance of a message unit that does not fit with the other elements that is cause for suspicion.

In the previous example, we saw a discordance between two messages that followed in sequence from different senders. The following illustrates this type of contradiction in a sequence of messages from a single communicator. Marvin has been told by his fiancée that he has impregnated her out of wedlock. In response, he states the following: "Don't worry, I really want to marry you. I love you very much. Everything will be all right. A friend of mine married a girl under these circumstances and then found out someone else had actually been the father."

Marvin's initial communications are straightforward and logical. While they may or may not express his true feelings, their failure to do so would be the result of deliberate distortion or lying.

On the other hand, the comment about the paternity issue is a thinly disguised, though automatically encoded, message that contains Marvin's raw doubts about his fiancée and *her* truthfulness. On a deeper level, it also reflects a fantasy-wish within Marvin that he is impotent and unable to impregnate anyone. In any case, it is this message, quite out of keeping with the other communicative units, that suggests the presence of unconscious encoding.

DISCORDANCE BETWEEN INTENDED AND RECEIVED MESSAGES

When the conscious intention and meaning assigned to a message by the sender are at variance with those implications detected by the receiver, the presence of an encoded communication may account for the discrepancy. However, under these circumstances especially the receiver must validate his or her interpretation of the received message. Suspicion may stem as readily from misunderstanding as from sound perception in such a case.

For example, Norma asks her fellow employee, Oscar, to have dinner with her. Oscar responds by asking her if she had mailed the letter he had dictated an hour ago.

Norma consciously decodes Oscar's response as reflecting an encoded message that she must keep her place as his secretary and not expect a social relationship and that he has no wish to have dinner with her. Upset, she responds by conveying these perceptions to him. He then denies that this is his intended meaning and stresses the importance of the letter he has referred to (because his job is at stake).

The situation is stalemated until we observe Oscar's further communications. If he begs off from dinner for one or another reason, Norma's perception has a greater likelihood of being valid. But if he accepts her invitation for dinner and responds with great warmth, we might be inclined to accept his explanation and to believe that he had intended no hidden meaning or that it was of minor consequence. We need supportive manifest and latent messages in making a decision as to whether an encoded message does indeed exist. Clarification of the context (here, the realization that Oscar was indeed coping with a trigger of which Norma was not aware) is often the basis on which this type of resolution can be made.

INEXPLICABLE ERRORS

The experience of any type of slip of the tongue, misperception, lapse of memory, blatant but temporary misunderstanding of others, and behavior that is not in keeping with one's conscious thoughts and intentions, are all signs of the use of encoded expression. All such lapses and unexplained behaviors are likely to be founded on, and therefore suggest, the presence of hidden meanings.

There is, for example, the well-known joke about the man who goes to buy two airline tickets to Pittsburgh and finds himself confronted with an extremely attractive and remarkably busty woman. Flustered, experiencing a confusion of sexual feelings, he says to her, "I'll take two pickets to Tittsburgh."

The slip of the tongue is an unconsciously encoded message that immediately reveals his sexual fantasy of possessing the young woman's breasts and perhaps as well of flying away with her. On a deeper level, there may also have been an unconscious perception of a measure of seductiveness in the ticket agent. In all, a slip of the tongue tends to reveal in relatively thinly disguised fashion an anxiety-provoking raw message, although upon analysis, it often contains as well additional encoded meanings.

This same man, at a time when his wife separated from him and locked him out of the apartment (for seemingly good reason: he was a terrible lady's man and flirt), inadvertently locked himself out of his car. Eventually, he was able to make a forced entry. The entire experience derived from his response to the trigger of his wife's action and conveyed his sense of outrage at being locked out of his apartment and his violent wishes to reenter his abode. On a deeper level, the encoded message involved wishes to assault and penetrate his wife.

HIGHLY CHARGED AND EMOTIONAL CONTENTS

As we have seen, any situation that is extremely conflicted or that involves intense emotions and personal feelings is likely to evoke the use of messages with important hidden meanings. This is especially true in the presence of anxiety and other disturbing affects, as well as when there is a sense of mistrust or danger.

The more our messages veer away from dealing with relatively neutral external realities, the more likely the presence of hidden messages. Efforts to deal with our own internal anxieties and conflicts are therefore likely to involve internal dialogues heavily laden with disguised communications. In practical terms, this means that such efforts at conflict resolution and coping should involve some work directed toward the decoding of their disguised messages. Without such measures, there is a severe limitation in the person's understanding of his or her own problems and of the best ways to effect their resolution.

EMOTIONAL SYMPTOMS

All types of psychologically founded symptoms such as phobias, obsessions, anxiety, and many forms of psychosomatic disorders are indicators of the presence of hidden messages. Symptoms are by definition discordant with or inappropriate to prevailing actualities and are therefore derived from and founded upon disguised and concealed inner messages.

For example, Peter suffers from a fear of elevators. In a dream, he is in an elevator with a man who is his age and who seems to be related to him in some way. The man tries to murder him by beating him to death.

In associating to this dream, Peter remembers that his mother told him of a miscarriage she had about a year before he was born. We could then suggest that through displacement (from the uterus to the elevator), and by means of symbolization (the elevator representing the womb and the man representing the lost fetus-sibling), Peter has revealed an unconscious fantasy that he was in the womb with this sibling who died and that he was responsible for killing him. Peter fears both his own violence and guilt-ridden impulses and revenge from the dead fetus. His fear of being in an elevator is a symptomatic expression of these underlying fantasies and beliefs. Recognizing their existence and their sources should help Peter begin to resolve his symptoms.

THE EMERGENCE OF SPECIAL MESSAGE FORMS

Throughout these discussions we have touched upon various types of messages that are likely to contain encoded meanings. To summarize, they include the following:

1. Emotional symptoms.
2. Slips of the tongue and symptomatic acts, as well as behaviors that are unexpected or discordant with conscious intentions.
3. Products of imagination, such as night dreams, stories, plays, daydreams, and myths, as well as paintings, musical compositions, sculpture, and poetry.
4. Messages that are illogical or disregard reality.
5. Messages with a notable measure of ambiguity.
6. Unexpected messages, or those that are discordant with the other messages in a sequence.
7. Richly imaginative messages and images.

It is to be stressed, however, that these message forms may or may not contain important encoded expressions, and that far more mundane and simplistic messages may nonetheless be used for important encoded communications. These are matters of likelihood; the specific determination depends, as always, on a recognition of the trigger and broad context for the particular message.

There are also certain kinds of settings and situations that are likely to foster the use of messages with important encoded meanings. Romantic and loving settings and those charged with destructiveness and danger have these qualities. Disturbing settings and experiences, such as hospitals, examinations, and acute traumas are of this kind. Ambiances related to creativity such as the theater or movies tend to have such qualities. The same is true of strange and bizarre settings and situations, and of any set of conditions under which our basic hold on reality is impaired.

There are, then, a number of different clues that suggest the presence of encoded communication. Studied carefully and with due caution, they facilitate understanding and response.

CHAPTER 10

DIRECT AND CONTEXTUAL (TRIGGER) DECODING

To the best of present-day knowledge, there is but one basic model of the decoding process. As noted, unconscious encoding is initiated by an emotionally meaningful stimulus or trigger, one that contains sufficient threat or evoked fantasy to lead to a defensive but adaptive processing that is in part outside of awareness and subjected to the primary-process mode of thinking. While Freud actually proposed this model in *The Interpretation of Dreams,* his analysis of these sequences tended to emphasize evoked fantasies (the intrapsychic realm) to the relative neglect of encoded perceptions (the interpersonal realm). This arose because he often failed to engage in a full analysis of the manifest and latent meanings of the trigger or day residue for a dream, or tended to emphasize those hidden implications of the stimulus for the dream that were evocative of fantasy reactions.

Freud's approach created a psychoanalytic tradition in which, for these many years, the overriding emphasis has been on the intrapsychic stirrings of the patient, including his or her transferences. Freud defined *transference* as an encoded fantasy within the patient that was derived from a disturbing or pathological early childhood relationship, one that has been (without due cause or stimulus) displaced onto the analyst. Virtually all that the patient experienced in the analytic situation was viewed as transference and therefore as fantasy; reality and perceptiveness were neglected. Interestingly, this particular overemphasis also derived from a failure to analyze fully how the analyst's interventions triggered the patient's responsive material. There was a striking neglect of the manifest and latent implications of these interventions, with a resultant failure to appreciate the extent to which the patient was responding with encoded but highly perceptive reactions to the analyst's effort. The fullness of the unconscious communicative interaction between patient and therapist simply was not sufficiently appreciated.

It is, of course, self-protective (and unfortunately, self-serving) for an analyst to disregard his or her unconsciously encoded messages to patients. This is so largely because it is at this level that the therapist expresses his or her own psychopathology or *countertransferences;* as a result, such disregard is a denial of disturbances and sickness in the therapist himself or herself.

This perspective helps to explain the neglect by analysts and others of trigger or *indirect* decoding. The human tendency is toward self-protection and defense; we tend to avoid this level of conscious understanding, which carries with it a large measure of anxiety and pain. We prefer to attend to manifest contents or to shift to *direct decoding*, in which we seek the hidden fantasies of the sender with no regard to his or her perceptiveness. There is a natural proclivity among both therapists and laypersons to think mainly of the fantasies communicated by other persons and to neglect their own disturbing fantasy systems and the encoded perceptions of themselves by others. Direct decoding is therefore extremely attractive in the large measure of protection it offers the decoder.

DIRECT DECODING

In direct decoding, use is made of knowledge of symbols, psychoanalytic theory, dynamics and genetics, the message sender in general, and his or her associations to the message itself. There is, however, no attempt to place the message involved in a broad context or to consistently analyze it as an adaptive response to a trigger or stimulus.

While this omission might appear on the surface to be of little consequence, empirically the situation turns out to be otherwise. It emerges that many triggers are far more disturbing and disruptive than realized and that in a large number of situations it is the decoder of the message who has also created the traumatic stimulus. Still, without a full comprehension of the trigger for a message, we are left with broad generalizations, speculations regarding fantasy, and clichés. Often we lack the ability to recognize specific evoked fantasies as well as the entire realm of valid but encoded perceptions. Because of this, many statements that are made about the sender of a message through direct decoding involve dynamics and genetics (childhood factors) that actually belong to the receiver and decoder of the message (assuming that he or she has indeed been a significant part of the trigger).

The following interchange will be used to illustrate direct decoding, and later, to contrast it with trigger decoding.

BETTY (a young child): I hate those television ads that those aspirin companies are making.

ED (her father): What do you hate about them?

BETTY: It's not fair. One company attacks all the other aspirin companies and says they're all bad.

ED: It's just their way of trying to sell their own brand of aspirin. They want you to think that their brand is better so they try to prove it to you.

BETTY: But it's not right to say the other aspirins are bad for you. They're not bad. If they keep saying that, no one will buy aspirin any more.

ED: Sure they will. They'll buy them because aspirins make headaches go away.

BETTY: But those ads spoil it for you. Then the aspirins won't work. I don't want to take aspirins ever again.

The qualities of this surface exchange are self-evident. This is a logical discussion between a child who dislikes a particular form of advertising and a father who is trying to offer a different perspective.

Are there any signs here of unconsciously encoded messages? We cannot be certain. There is no clear indication of encoding, although there is a hint of it in Betty's somewhat *magical thinking*—i.e., that aggressive ads will render aspirins ineffective. The aspirin advertisement is a creative product, and it could well be lending itself here to some type of encoded expression. In all, this is the kind of situation in which, if nothing more were known, we might be inclined to accept these messages at face value and not engage in any type of decoding effort. Many people consider this type of advertising in poor taste and are disturbed by its hostile qualities. There is no inherent reason to believe that this attitude is based on unconscious images.

INFERENCES AND IMAGES

A great deal of direct decoding involves self-evident *inferences* contained in messages. General themes and meanings are identified and often stated intellectually. Specific *images* and *narratives* (fantasies or perceptions) are not used, and the formulations are rather flat. This type of decoding is relatively simple to carry out even though it seldom touches upon a true unconscious raw message because these are always expressed in image or narrative rather than inference form. We must therefore distinguish between a formulation that involves a direct inference (an inference derivative) and that which involves an image or narrative (in short, an image derivative). As noted earlier, a derivative is any manifest message that is considered to contain at least one or more encoded messages. The manifest message is derived from the underlying message and therefore functions as a derivative of the latent content. Decoding itself involves derivations moving from the surface to the depths.

INFERENCE DECODING

In this first form of direct decoding, then, there is the development of general themes and inference derivatives. For example, it would be proposed that Betty is feeling angry ("I hate these television ads"). She is concerned with fairness and rivalry, the attack of one company on another. Later on, she is worried about badness and about a bad image that will lead her to avoid aspirin. Since aspirin is a curative drug, it seems she is concerned that something potentially helpful will be spoiled.

There is, indeed, a thin yield of understanding from the use of inference derivatives. Nonetheless, for some decoders these efforts would generate a sense that Betty is dealing with issues of hostility, rivalry and competition, goodness and badness, and some sense that a therapeutic effect has been spoiled. Many would believe that some meaningful understanding has been arrived at in this way. The thinness and emptiness of this process and its results would be ignored.

A second and related step in inference decoding is to study the *sequence* of a group of messages and their implications. It is correctly proposed that there is some unconscious thread that links one message to the other, though the use of this principle is often in error.

To speculate here, it may well be that the sequence suggests that Betty is struggling with her own sense of hostility and trying to manage it by telling herself that feeling angry is a bad way to be. If she keeps it up, no one will want to have anything to do with her.

It is possible to combine the study of sequence with direct efforts at symbolic decoding. This too is a way of developing inference derivatives, although they sometimes involve isolated images as well. For example, the allusion to the television may imply themes of voyeurism; in this light, the speculation might be that Betty is angry over something she has seen. A psychoanalyst might pick up this thread and suggest that the next message implies that Betty has seen something that she had experienced as an attack by one person on another. When Betty states that it is wrong, this would be seen as an expression of conscience, and the concept of the *superego* would be invoked. Finally, whatever Betty has seen has spoiled something curative for her.

In general, the development of inference derivatives is flat, clichéd, and limited. If Betty had reported watching a child trapped in a room, we might postulate an intrauterine fantasy. If she spoke of a tall building that had been knocked to the ground, we could suggest bodily anxieties and even fantasies of having been castrated (the loss of the fantasied penis) or wishing to castrate (her father in this instance, since he is the recipient of the message). When direct decoding yields seemingly powerful and disturbing inferences of this kind, it is thought to be valid and useful. The flaws go unrecognized.

SYMBOLIC (DIRECT) DECODING

Implicit in direct decoding is a measure of displacement. Whatever Betty saw that disturbed her was not on the television, but elsewhere. In this particular message sequence, the nature of the displacement cannot be identified. If we question Betty and she mentions seeing her parents fight, we would then have a better sense of a possible displaced and encoded meaning for these messages. But in that case, we would have identified the trigger for Betty's communications and be in a position to formulate an abundance of encoded perceptions as well as responsive fantasies.

On the other hand, if Betty connected these messages to a dream she had had of hitting someone while others watched, we would propose conflicts within her regarding hostile impulses and suggest that the voyeuristic trend actually represents an underlying exhibitionistic need—Betty's wish to expose her hostility and badness.

Finally, the allusion to aspirin, a pill taken by mouth, could suggest the presence of oral conflicts and concerns about taking in and incorporating. The imaginative individual might think of the aspirin as *the good mother*—i.e., the available maternal breast and mother's milk. If bitter taste were at issue, aspirin could simultaneously represent a bad breast, hurtful and bitter. Medications, doctors, and other caring figures might be involved on a latent level. The speculation might be to the effect that Betty has some conflict regarding oral incorporation and being cared for, and perhaps in some way she has a fantasy that these caring qualities have been spoiled for her.

In carrying out direct decoding, we tend to be prepared to find several fantasies compressed into a single message. We anticipate the use of displacement and symbolization and expect to find the presence of secondary revision and concerns for representability. In principle, we take a manifest message and attempt to develop the general themes so contained and to translate the specific symbols involved from their manifest representations to underlying raw message meanings. Direct decoding is more easily applied to products of the imagination such as dreams than to message sequences such as those between Betty and her father. It will therefore be further illustrated in a subsequent chapter. For the moment, the stress has been on the limitations of such efforts and the strong possibility that they can lead to false impressions.

If Ed had limited himself to direct decoding, he might have developed the belief that his daughter was disturbed by something, perhaps the television ad itself or something else. He would be able to recognize his daughter's concern with uncontrolled hostility and competition and with some type of badness. He would realize that something good and helpful was being spoiled for her, and he would try to reassure her. Sensing some type of displacement and symbolic representation, he might then ask his daughter some questions in the hope that the underlying issues might emerge. As noted, quite often this leads to the discovery of the trigger for the sequence at hand and immediately reveals the key displacements involved. Since this shift is from direct to trigger decoding, let us now move on to the particular topic.

CONTEXTUAL OR TRIGGER DECODING

There is, of course, some excitement in translating symbols and in speculating about another person's terrible fantasies. Nonetheless, many of the objections to armchair analysts and therapists (and to professional therapists as well) have arisen from their arbitrary use of direct decoding. If something can mean virtually anything else, who is to say what it really means? The individual with the greatest authority or charisma usually holds sway.

Trigger decoding brings a sense of certainty to the arbitrary qualities of direct decoding. It is a decoding procedure that is highly personal, quite specific, and immediately pertinent to ongoing interactions and relationships. Because it involves a powerful guiding force, it has definitive qualities lacking with other types of decoding; it far more readily produces a sense of conviction in both the unwitting sender and the decoding receiver. Trigger decoding is also at once alive and adaptive. As such, its conscious accomplishment is extremely helpful in coping with oneself and others.

With direct decoding, it is necessary to make many assumptions regarding the operation of the primary-process mechanisms. Displacement is assumed and is pursued, as in condensation, symbolization, and the rest. In contrast, with contextual decoding the first and key step is the identification of the trigger. Once the nature of the stimulus for a message is known in depth, the transformations created by the primary-process mode of mentation are relatively easy to identify. A fairly arbitrary decoding process is replaced with one that is definitive.

Throughout our lives, we respond to emotionally laden triggers with conscious and unconscious reactions. The direct and conscious adjustment may be adaptive or maladaptive, appropriate or inappropriate. When it is reasonable and sensible, it reflects a measure of coping that is under the individual's direct control. When the response is inappropriate or symptomatic, we have a situation where unconscious factors must be taken into account. An emotional disturbance is, by definition, a communicative response to a trigger that is not entirely in keeping with the realities involved and which derives some of its inappropriate qualities from unconsciously encoded perceptions and fantasies.

In a sense, then, when things are going smoothly, we need not be concerned about our own encoded messages. It is mainly when under emotional stress that we are well advised to make continual efforts to decode the messages we send and those we receive from others.

Contextual decoding begins with a particular communication that appears to contain an important encoded expression. We then identify its trigger and subject it to analysis. If possible, the earlier trigger for that particular trigger can be identified as a way of maintaining a broader perspective. However, to simplify this discussion, we will concentrate on only a small portion of this type of sequence.

The trigger is something like a decoding key. All encoded reactions must in some way reflect their stimuli. Each trigger shapes a responsive message along very specific lines. The trigger and a reactive communication are like the cogs of an interlocking pair of wheels or an antigen and antibody: one shapes the other. Sometimes, in fact, we will know only a responsive message and not the trigger and yet be able to offer some rather cogent speculations as to the possible stimuli for the message itself. At other times, aspects of the message remind us of a dimension of a trigger that we have overlooked. Similarly, a full sense of the nature of a particular precipitant or stimulus helps us to anticipate certain types of encoded reactions.

Returning now to the dialogue between Betty and Ed, it will be of interest to hypothesize two different triggers for this exchange. Each will lead to an effort at decoding with a somewhat different (though somewhat interrelated) outcome. Each will provide a chance to practice the decoding process and to identify the steps involved.

TWO TRIGGERS FOR ONE SCENE ───────────────

ONE TRIGGER: A SPANKING

As a first example, let us suppose that just an hour or so earlier Ed had yelled at and spanked Betty's brother, Victor. With this as the immediate trigger, how would you decode the hidden messages in their dialogue?

We might begin with an analysis of the manifest and latent meanings of the trigger. For Betty, the trigger involved a perception of her father as unfairly punitive because she had sided with her brother and saw his prank as rather innocuous. On another level, the act had gratified an unconscious hostile fantasy within Betty that involved harming her brother. Finally, her brother was seen as the victim of an assault against which he was relatively helpless. (While there are other dimensions to this trigger, we will confine ourselves to these three.)

We may now select highlights of Betty's messages and decode their meanings. Betty's opening communication is to the effect that it is not fair when one company attacks another. Immediately, we know that *displacement* has taken place: the scene has shifted from Betty's father and brother to the television advertisement. We might suggest that Betty is fearful of being hit by her father and that the spanking had made her quite anxious. As a result, she has criticized her father through encoded rather than far more dangerous direct messages. All the while, she is quite unaware of her image of her father and her resentment toward him. On a conscious level, she has already completely forgotten the incident with her brother (i.e., repression has set in).

Betty finds a means of representing her brother's spanking that is well disguised and somewhat distant from her conscious and unconscious perceptions of her father. And yet, Betty has found a rather effective but indirect way of letting her father know that she resents aggressors who attack others for being bad. Typically, the message is directed toward the individual who triggered the expression and whom it concerns, though on the surface there is no allusion whatsoever to either Betty's father or brother. Through encoded messages, Betty has made her anger and disillusionment quite clear. Through displacement, symbolization (and condensation and secondary revision), Betty warns her father that if he continues these hostile behaviors, she will alienate herself from him.

IDENTIFY AND ANALYZE THE TRIGGER

This is the essence of trigger decoding. We identify the trigger, formulate its main direct and indirect meanings and functions, and consider the consequent manifest messages. These messages are derivatives or disguised versions of the trigger and of the receiver's reactions to it. Through condensation, Betty's messages are an attempt to deal first with the threatening and hostile message from her father, and second, with her own aggressive impulses toward her brother.

On this latter level, Betty is experiencing an *unconscious* internal dialogue in that its most important meanings are outside of her awareness. Certainly, there is a conscious struggle over advertising practices. But in Betty's emotional life and development, this concern about advertising is a displaced and encoded way of working over and resolving her guilt over her secret gratification in her brother's beating. Toward the end of this dialogue, then, we see Betty reminding herself in encoded fashion that her hostility will spoil her relationship with her brother and that she had best get it under control.

Betty had been relatively quiet after the spanking until she had seen the television ad. Consciously, the ad had fascinated and disturbed her. Unconsciously, she had found a strong communicative vehicle with which to work over the conflicts which the spanking had triggered.

Had Betty's father been aware of the important emotional trigger for these messages from Betty, and had he been sensitive to trigger decoding, he might have suspected that there was more to Betty's concern about the advertising issue. He would then have cast about identifying the general themes (hatred, unfair attacks, saying other people are bad, rejection) and then have made an attempt to identify an emotionally important trigger that would fit well with these general threads. If he were insightful, he would have come to the spanking of his son. He then would have been able to shade the conversation over toward problems between fathers and children and offer a clearer explanation to his daughter. In this way, he might have been able to help her work over her reactions to the incident on a conscious level, rather than allowing them to remain quite unconscious and uncertain in their direction. Conscious insight is the ultimate sign of mastery; it offers the greatest likelihood that a conflict, perception, or fantasy will be resolved in the best possible manner.

Notice too how our earlier, uncertain impressions, derived from direct decoding, have now taken on a far more specific, personal, and surprisingly meaningful set of qualities. Once a trigger has been identified, the first available message should be examined and decoded in light of its meanings. If displacement, condensation, and symbolism appear to be in operation and an apparently meaningful raw image message discovered, one should move on from there to the next message unit. If the first formulation was correct, this second message unit should lend it fresh support. A meaningful sequence of messages does indeed offer a series of encoded perceptions and fantasies, each of which has a somewhat different slant—one moment a perception, the next a fantasy, the next a connection to early childhood, the next a different level of interrelated meaning, and so on. We call this a *coalescible set of derivatives,* a set of expressed hidden meanings which illuminate different dimensions of a trigger. This accumulation of diversely pertinent meanings is one of the ways in which we attempt to validate our own decoding efforts.

Condensed into these messages is Betty's mixed image of her father as a helpful parent who has done something hostile and destructive. Since Betty's evaluation of the situation appears to be quite accurate (it was a friend of her brother who had misbehaved and not her brother), this is an encoded but *valid* unconscious perception. On another level, not previously mentioned, Betty identified with her brother and imagined herself receiving the spanking. In itself, this is a reactive fantasy with which Betty continued to struggle, working it over through her encoded messages.

It is important to stress again that unconscious fantasies and perceptions are known to exist only because they manifest themselves through surface communications which contain their portrayal and meanings in disguised form. We are not dealing here with mysterious unrepresented and unfathomable processes and contents. We are dealing with communicative expressions and defenses against their *direct* realization.

The search for triggers is guided, even unconsciously, by the messages we are receiving. Much of it depends on an understanding of human nature and of the types of communications that disturb or arouse others. When someone seems perturbed or has shifted to encoded communication, we must carefully search our own behavior and expressions for important evocative emotional stimuli. Contextual decoding depends upon an accurate identification of the most critical triggers for a person's encoded communications and of the most vital meanings of each stimulus. It is important in this regard to not overlook a highly traumatic trigger by suggesting that a far more innocuous stimulus is involved. Our knowledge of others depends to a large extent on our understanding of ourselves and the nature of emotional traumas.

This point is illustrated here by the way in which Betty's father took the television ad per se as the trigger for her messages. As such, it hardly lends itself to the decoding of Betty's subsequent communications. It required considerably more sensitivity to realize that Betty's messages contained within them, first and foremost, an encoded representation of a trigger to which she could not allude directly.

In some situations, individuals do mention highly charged triggers briefly and in passing, a sufficient (and ideal) direct representation that should alert the listener to the key stimulus for what is to follow. At other times, especially when it is the listener who has created the trigger and who is viewed as highly dangerous, the trigger will not be mentioned manifestly but referred to in encoded fashion. Still, in every situation, one should seek out the most traumatic recent incidents. In addition, if an identified trigger is not facilitating the decoding process, the search must be made for a different stimulus. It is well to realize that in this area we are working against a defensive need that will lead us to deny our most hurtful expressions and to avoid the deeper meanings of recognized precipitants. Trigger decoding begins with a deep and honest scrutiny of one's own feelings and behaviors.

A SECOND TRIGGER: A DIVORCE

Let us suppose now that the trigger for these messages involved the pending divorce of Betty's parents. Earlier that day, Betty had been with her mother and was exposed to a tirade of criticism of her father. Later on, the father had more subtly and through encoded messages attacked her mother in turn. With these incidents as the stimulus, how would we decode Betty's messages?

In this instance, we have not described the trigger in detail but simply afforded it a central characterization. While Betty had not entirely forgotten the experience with her mother, it was certainly not on her mind consciously as she spoke about the television ads. Nonetheless, the trigger of her mother's attacks on her father makes these messages relatively easy to decode. By undoing the use of displacement (from Betty's mother and father to two opposing aspirin companies) and symbolization (the advertising issue is used to portray the struggle between Betty's parents), we are able to recognize that Betty had found a rather exquisite way of letting her father know just how unhappy she is over the efforts of each of her parents to attack the other. With an encoded warning, she tells her father that if the battle continues, her relationship with both parents will be spoiled and she will not want to be with them again.

These were truly painful messages for this child (and her father), and yet they needed expression—partly to help Betty work through the trauma and partly as a way of letting her father know on some level how upsetting the situation was for her. It is in light of this trigger that the symbolic use of aspirin, a somewhat unpleasant form of nurturing, takes on symbolic meaning as a representation of Betty's parents and their caring functions.

Had Betty's father recognized the trigger for these communications and understood the encoded messages, he might have engaged in a dialogue with his daughter through the use of deliberate conscious encoding of his own. He might have explained to her that sometimes aspirin companies don't realize that they are hurting their competitors, adding that they really mean well despite the hurtful things they say. He might have agreed with his daughter that it is not right to fault others. Then, too, he might have said that sometimes things that help you feel better, and even people who do so, can be hurtful and spoil the effect. He might have told her that people are mixtures of good and hurtful impulses, and especially when they are upset themselves or forcefully directed toward a particular goal, they may be more hurtful than they mean to be.

In this way, a proper trigger decoding of Betty's messages could have led to a very apt encoded response, one that Ed's daughter could have registered unconsciously and even translated into some conscious realizations. Ed could have helped his daughter to cope with a very difficult situation. But in his failure to recognize the encoded meanings of her messages, Ed fell quite short of offering a helpful response.

VALIDATION IN SOCIAL SETTINGS

No discussion of trigger decoding is complete without a recognition of the need to find some way to validate a budding formulation. Because of the natural tendencies to overinvest in one's own impressions and to develop them in keeping with personal defensive needs, the possibilities of bias and distortion are enormous. To safeguard against these pressures, the search for confirmation must be constant. Simultaneously, it is essential to maintain an openness to the lack of validation and to recognize indications that a particular line of thought is not gaining support from an ongoing analysis of an unfolding sequence of messages.

In social situations, the available options for validation are rather limited. The following are the best resources for this type of effort.

PREDICTION

As soon as a listener feels that he or she is receiving a sequence of encoded messages, there should be a shift to trigger decoding. The first step, as we know, involves identifying the stimulus for the message sequence. Next, the manifest and latent meanings of the trigger itself are identified and catalogued. At that point, the work of decoding the ongoing messages in light of their precipitants can be initiated.

If one moves quickly enough, certain very specific trends, themes, and encoded meanings are soon in evidence. It is then possible to anticipate as yet unexpressed encoded messages that are likely to emerge in light of the trigger and the existent encoded expressions. When these anticipations are fulfilled, we have a particularly powerful form of validation for our original hypotheses and formulations. Nonetheless, because of the enormous vulnerability to prejudice of the decoding process, and the great need for self-confirmation, even this sense of validation must be carefully reexamined and tested out before we can feel confident that a piece of decoding has been accurate and successful.

In the material cited above, the formulation that Betty was attempting through encoded messages to comment on her parents' hostility toward each other found only minimal support in the dialogue presented earlier. There is indeed some elaboration of themes related to anger and destruction, but little in the way of unique realizations that would confirm this particular hypothesis. However, such validation did emerge when just a few minutes later Betty suddenly thought of Michael, the little boy who had played with her brother.

Michael's parents were also getting divorced. Betty suddenly described how Michael's mother says all these mean things about his father, and what a no-good man he is. Betty feels this is unfair to both Michael and his father, and confided in her own father that Michael was thinking of running away from home.

Through these far less disguised yet still encoded messages (here, there is a major use of displacement and only a minimal use of symbolism), we find strong support for our initial formulations. In light of this evidence, Betty's father, Ed, would be well advised to discuss these issues with his daughter—directly or indirectly.

On rare occasions, the breakthrough of the very message a decoder believes to be present in a series of manifest communications can also be taken as a validation of an initial formulation. However, since we are usually dealing with strongly defended messages, this type of validation must be subjected to careful reassessment since it may be more misleading than confirmatory. One can have more confidence in this kind of confirmation after engaging in conscious decoding in response to a detected encoded message, and discovering that the sender eventually expresses the formulated hidden message rather directly.

THE APPEARANCE OF LESS AND LESS DISGUISED DERIVATIVES

As we know, threatening messages are often heavily encoded and quite removed from their manifest (raw) expressions. There is a great distance between the raw image and the disguised communication.

There are, however, certain sequences in which an initial message is decoded in light of its trigger, and subsequent messages, less and less disguised, support an initial formulation. We saw an example of this kind just a moment ago when Betty spoke of her brother's friend. This type of gradual lessening of defense is typical in situations where a sender feels a growing sense of safety and feels understood by his or her receiver. Much therefore depends on the receiver's direct and encoded responses. As a rule, any attempt to break down the defenses used by the sender, such as stating outright the raw message that he or she is disguising, will tend to increase rather than decrease the sender's need for direct denial and for further heavily encoded messages. A receiver can create a sense of safety and protection in his or her relationship with a sender in far more effective fashion through the use of responsive, consciously encoded messages that reveal a sense of understanding without direct confrontation. In general, it is this type of rejoinder that will lead a sender to gradually lessen his or her use of defensive disguise and to arrive on his or her own at a more open and, eventually, undisguised expression of the raw messages at hand.

COALESCING DERIVATIVES

A sequence of communications which supports an initial formulation through the emergence of a series of derivative messages that touch upon different meanings and dimensions of the implications of a specific trigger constitute a form of encoded confirmation of an original hypothesis. This quality of diverse and coalescible meanings implies that at one moment there is an encoded perception, while next there is an encoded fantasy, soon followed by an allusion to some connection with the past (a genetic tie) and then perhaps an attempt at generating a coping reaction. Should this type of multifaceted and diverse accumulation of encoded meaning organize cogently around the meanings of an identified trigger, the decoding effort and formulation are likely to be quite valid.

Suppose that after Betty spoke about her brother's friend and his parents, she suddenly remembered a time when she was taken to a hospital for a tonsillectomy. She thought mainly of being left by her parents and her great fear of being alone. Here, we would have an encoded genetic connection which reflects Betty's perception of the present situation as one in which she is in danger again of being abandoned by both of her parents. Her fear would be intensified by the efforts of each spouse to destroy the other, and by their insensitivities to Betty's needs. This is a *transversal communication* in that it expresses (transverses) both a strong sense of unconscious perception and a notable measure of unconscious fantasy (the fear/wish to be separated from her parents). This particular element, taken together with Betty's earlier encoded communications (which contain a number of different perceptions and fantasies), produces a divergent but coalescible derivative complex that strongly supports the initial formulation of Betty's encoded messages. This speaks for validation of the hypothesis.

A UNIQUE COMMUNICATION

In a type of validation in which a unique communication is followed by the offer of a formulation to the message sender, the receiver actually attempts to *interpret* the encoded meanings of a sender's message in light of a significant trigger. This particular intervention is designed to account for a symptom or emotional disturbance by identifying the trigger which has set it off and the encoded meanings (perceptions and fantasies) which account for its *underlying* (unconscious) structure. Fundamental to interpretation is the effort to make conscious some content or process in a sender who has not previously been aware of them. However, in keeping with our redefinition of the decoding process, we must redefine the concept of interpretation so that it always is organized in terms of encoded reactions to a meaningful trigger.

It is here that once again an enormous need for caution is required. The listener to an encoded message is not a therapist and in general does not have the responsibility of interpreting hidden meanings to a sender. There is no doubt that some social relationships involve strong unconscious and therapeutic qualities, although only rarely are these sought on a direct and manifest level. There is a disturbance in communication whenever an individual adopts a role that is discordant with conscious and unconscious expectations and with the basic context and nature of the prevailing relationship.

Because of this, the best kind of interpretation is made indirectly, through conscious encoding. Rather than stating a specific hypothesized meaning for a particular encoded message, the receiver shapes a response that takes this hidden meaning into account. If the sender then reveals a unique message that adds to the meaning of the formulation at hand, validation is in evidence. This is more likely to occur after indirect (encoded) rather than conscious (direct) interpretation because of the great defensive needs of the sender who encodes his or her messages.

At times, it is indeed possible to offer a direct interpretation, although it must be done with tact and by citing all of the available evidence. After all, the sender has encoded his or her message because of fear and anxiety; a direct interpretation is an attempt to bypass or break down the defenses involved. Depending on the relationship, the nature of the messages involved, and a number of other factors, the sender may or may not directly acknowledge the listener's hypothesis even if it is essentially correct. However, the most crucial type of validation in response to a conscious interpretation inevitably must involve a fresh *encoded* message. Thus, true confirmation occurs only when the sender suddenly remembers a previously forgotten (repressed) message (dream, incident, or whatever) which contains within it, in encoded form, a new and truly unique element that enlarges the proferred formulation.

Suppose in the situation between Betty and her father, Ed had responded (as described before) with a series of consciously encoded messages through which he tried to help his daughter understand the stress affecting both him and his wife and through which he offered both a new perspective and an apology. If Betty had then mentioned her mother's tirade against her father and directly described her feelings of anger and upset, she would have provided an initial confirmation of the hypothesis about the meaning of her encoded messages. If she had then remembered a dream in which a woman was stabbing a man, she would have provided a form of encoded validation that would justify additional confidence in our initial formulation.

A DELICATE BALANCE

It is important, then, to maintain a balance between the acceptance of surface messages and the use of trigger decoding. Those who tend to adhere to the surface of messages in the presence of disguised communication tend to be overly naive, concrete, unimaginative, and dull. Those who tend to neglect the surface and overinterpret supposed encoded meanings tend to be at the mercy of their own imaginations, to have difficulty in reacting to simple reality situations, and to be overly suspicious and even paranoid. There is a delicate balance between reading too much meaning into the messages of others and reading too little. The use of validating measures is an important safeguard against these difficulties.

Trigger decoding should be used wisely for understanding oneself and others. It is extremely useful in analyzing one's own dreams (as we will see in Part II) and in clarifying perplexing emotionally charged situations. On the other hand, one needs the utmost tact and sensitivity to offer these insights to a message sender. One should do so only rarely and under special circumstances, and one should realize that there is likely to be much responsive resistance. The impact of this type of decoding should not be underestimated; it can often be cataclysmic. As much as one would like to share his or her understanding with others, the risks often outweigh the gains. Quiet understanding is often the wiser course. And yet, in a moment of crisis, a cogent effort at trigger decoding can often clarify an otherwise chaotic situation. Ultimately, sound personal judgment must prevail.

PART II
HIDDEN MESSAGES IN OUR DAILY LIVES

CHAPTER 11

THE DIRECT DECODING OF DREAMS

Dreams are among the most consistent carriers of encoded messages. Considerable self-awareness can be derived from the analysis of dreams as long as we carry it out in light of day residues, or triggers, and their implications. Often we do this analysis in the quiet of an evening or while we lie in bed before going to sleep. The dreamer should adopt an attitude of free and loose association rather than attempting to directly decode the dream in intellectualized fashion. By initially allowing himself or herself a free sway of associations to the dream elements, the trigger for the dream will usually emerge in rather spontaneous fashion. In addition, there will be many other associations which constitute complementary encoded messages related to the dream experience. When the effort is successful, the dream and associations provide a direct representation of the trigger and a series of coalescible (encoded) derivatives. At some point, then, the dreamer can shift from free thoughts and images to an analysis of the material that he or she has conjured up. By organizing the communicative material in terms of triggers and encoded responses, one can develop considerable insight.

In *The Interpretation of Dreams*, Freud tended to concentrate his efforts on the dream itself rather than on the trigger or precipitant. Because of this, analysts think of associations to dreams rather than reactions to triggers. However, associations to dreams tend to foster formulations in terms of isolated encoded fantasies and to disregard interactions and encoded perceptions. Associations to triggers leave room for both types of responses; in general, perceptions prevail when a trigger is traumatic, and fantasies are relatively more active when a trigger is constructive and helpful.

The dream itself is a response to a trigger and is therefore simply a part of the associational network. While dreams are often highly meaningful, this need not always be the case (see Part III). Still, the shift from the view of the dream as the organizer of the patient's material to one in which the trigger is seen as the central factor is essential for proper decoding and understanding.

In the altered state of consciousness known as sleep there are important changes in our mental functioning that are conducive to the development of meaningful encoded messages. Waking defenses are modified, logic and reality largely set to the side, and there is a shift to primary-process mentation that permits the fluid flow of ideas and images.

A dream is first and foremost an encoded, self-directed communication. A dream may also be intended for the ears of others, and there is evidence that anyone to whom a dreamer tells his or her dream is part of the intended audience for the dream. In this section, we will study the dream as a means of further clarifying and solidifying our use of trigger decoding.

A DREAMER AND HIS DREAM

Bill dreamt that he was in bed with his friend Rodger and Rodger's girlfriend Sally. Sally looked kind of dirty, and Rodger had a moustache. Bill at first felt stimulated and wanted to get involved with Sally sexually, but he then pulled away. Naked, he walked toward the bathroom, passing the kitchen where his brother, Ken, was having breakfast. Ken seemed surprised to see him and looked almost dumbfounded, very perplexed. Bill reached the bathroom and, looking in the mirror he noticed a mole on his arm. The shade was up, and he pulled it down. A man came into the apartment with some secrets to sell. He was a spy or a blackmailer, and when Bill wanted no part of what he had to offer, they began to fight.

The following morning, Bill awoke with a clear recollection of his dream. He was confused on several points. His image of

Sally was uncertain. She was wearing a see-through negligee, that was for sure. But he had a vague impression that there was blood on the sheets and that Sally was menstruating. Despite all efforts to be certain of the entire dream, that particular image remained unclear.

At first, Bill felt puzzled. Sally was an attractive young woman, but did he really want to go to bed with her? If so, why put Rodger in the bed as well? And why of all things would he dream about Ken, whom he hadn't seen for some time? Why the mole on his arm and the blackmailer? Who in the world was he and why the fight?

This particular dream had been subjected to secondary revision that had allowed for the necessity of meaningful surface representation. It contained a logical sequence of events and images, although none of them made immediate sense to the dreamer, Bill. Experiences of this kind, and an inability to immediately detect the direct and implied meanings of a dream, suggest the presence of heavily encoded messages. Bill had an immediate sense that many of these images were laden with meaning; he sensed the dream's richness without knowing the specifics. Many of the elements were actually disquieting, another indication of encoding, and another motive for Bill to try to decode the dream.

RESPONDING TO THE SURFACE OF THE DREAM ———

Bill was a sophisticated young man who had had some practice in decoding his dreams. As he went about the business of getting ready to go to work, he attempted to engage in efforts at direct decoding, fully aware that these were insufficient. He recognized that he had dreamt of a threesome and that he was conflicted about his involvement with Sally. The mole on his arm implied some kind of mark or damage and could reflect some castration anxiety. The secrets or spy or blackmailer spoke for some kind of paranoid fantasy, while the fight suggested some type of hostile struggle with a man. Then, too, the blood on the sheets brought up the theme of bodily damage. Was there a fantasy related to the primal scene (observations of parental intercourse) accompanied by feelings of stimulation and guilt and by images of punishment through castration? Was there also some image of his mother as damaged, and was his brother in the dream because of some stirrings related to sibling rivalry? For Bill, these formulations had a clichéd quality; they were flat and empty, despite some of their seemingly primitive qualities. Even identifying the issues of exhibitionism and voyeurism seemed to go nowhere.

At times previously unconscious perceptions and fantasies appear manifestly in our dreams because of the lessening of defensive barriers. Although these are often the source of some insight, they must be accepted with caution; a far more critical function of a manifest dream involves the use of these images as a response to an emotional trigger designed to convey a message on an *encoded* level that remains outside of awareness. Dream elements often serve these dual functions: the representation of a previously repressed idea or image and the encoded expression of a somewhat different and still unconscious thought or feeling.

In this instance, prior to the dream, Bill had experienced no conscious attraction to Sally and had not thought of having sexual relations with her. Nevertheless, the dream image, which emphasized her allure, enabled him to recognize an attraction that had not previously registered. At the same time, the allusion to Sally looking dirty led Bill to recognize that there was something unkempt about her that made her a bit repugnant. In all, then, these manifest dream elements contained a direct representation of previously unconscious perceptions (of Sally's attractiveness and unattractiveness) and a fantasy-wish (of going to bed with her).

Realizations of this kind point to another reason for allowing oneself a chance to respond to the surface of a dream and to engage in efforts at direct decoding. Certain previously hidden fantasies and perceptions may emerge, as may a general sense of the nature of some intrapsychic or interpersonal experience that is currently active. This type of direct decoding, in which general themes are identified, may even suggest (point to) as yet unnoticed triggers for the dream itself. While direct decoding does not usually produce a definitive narrative and statement of underlying images and messages (perceptions and fantasies), it may point toward areas of general concern: here, for example, some type of sexual wish, some fear of bodily damage, exhibitionistic and/or voyeuristic needs, some concern with sibling rivalry, and a sense of issues related to dishonesty and guilt.

Little more is to be gained by proposing possible displacements. In suggesting a shift away from a traumatic primal scene experience, we still lack a sense of Bill's immediate struggle and its specific details. Proposing that there is an "oedipal triangle" between Bill and his parents that is represented through displacement in the dream of Bill, Rodger, and Sally, is to identify a universal unconscious struggle (a child's love for the parent of the opposite sex and his or her rivalry with the parent of the same sex) whose specific meaning, once more, eludes us. The same applies to the "orality" (mouth-oriented needs) suggested in Ken's eating and to the suggestion that the spy or blackmailer may be an evil (bad) representation of Bill's father.

All too often formulations of this kind are more the product of the imagination of the decoder—even if it is the message sender himself or herself—than they are of the intentions of the encoder. There is virtually no way to validate their presence. There is no way to ascertain their immediate role in Bill's life. More often than not, they actually serve as a kind of *fiction* created by the listener that is unconsciously designed to avoid the recognition of far more chaotic messages that would emerge through trigger decoding. In such situations, statements theoretically valid or true are used *functionally* as fictions or lies designed to cover over far more disturbing truths. Thus, they are statements that seem sound, but they are misapplied or irrelevant to the dynamics of the immediate moment.

The fact that these formulations are in keeping with an elaborate set of psychoanalytic postulates has deceived many individuals—patients, therapists, and others—and led them to believe that they must be inherently sound. It is of course a logical fallacy to suggest that because a statement has a dynamic meaning, it has been applied accurately and properly to the right person at the right moment. The statement that the sun rises in the east is true, while the statement that the sunrise was the cause of Bill's dream is patently false. Thus, statements of psychodynamics may be theoretically true in themselves, while their application to a specific moment and individual may be quite unfounded.

Because of the tendency for formulations of this kind to degenerate into jargon and psychoanalytic clichés, they must be made tentatively and with full recognition of their limitations. They are best used to foster some type of immediate understanding and to elicit additional evident inferences of the dream as part of the search for its triggers.

Even the proposition that every figure in a dream stands in some way for the dreamer himself or herself does little to change this characteristic of direct decoding. To suggest, for example, that Sally represents the feminine side of Bill is to generate a statement that involves the universal truth of the bisexuality that exists in all of us. To add that Bill's feminine image is a mixed one with attributes of attractiveness, dirtiness, exhibitionism, and bloodiness is to identify a further universal conflict that exists in virtually everyone's identity. Even the proposal that the dream suggests that this particular conflict is especially prominent in Bill does little to tell us what has set off this conflict, how Bill is dealing with it, what it means to him, or how it is affecting him at present. It is easy to be lulled into this type of formulation.

We can offer the same objections to any attempt to identify early childhood figures in this dream. Quite obviously, Sally could represent Bill's mother and Rodger his father. One can even suggest that the father is represented twice over: as the sexual Rodger and as the threatening spy or blackmailer. These are all truths without definitive content. Like a man without a country, they float haplessly about, without roots or meaning.

In our direct decoding, we have of course been taking into account in a general way the postulated operation of displacement, condensation, and symbolism—now familiar mechanisms. Direct decoding is carried out by looking for other figures and situations which could be portrayed in encoded form by the manifest dream and reflected in its general themes.

Whatever truths are contained in this type of direct translation, they are relatively insignificant compared to those arrived
at through trigger decoding. Rather than pursuing the many
other possible inferences and directly decoded messages that
could be derived from this dream, let us now move on to
trigger decoding.

CHAPTER 12

THE TRIGGER DECODING OF DREAMS

As we know, trigger decoding begins with a search for the day residues or stimuli that prompt a particular dream. Often, there are several important triggers, and the main problem becomes a matter of characterizing the manifest and latent implications of each precipitant and selecting those that have had the most powerful influence. At times, we are directly aware of a disturbing experience and can immediately turn to a dream as a way of detecting some initial evident encoded reactions. Subsequently, these can then be extended with additional associations.

On the other hand, as in the situation in the preceding chapter with Bill, there are times when we are unable to think immediately of a particular trigger. We turn to the manifest dream itself, as well as to efforts at direct decoding, for clues as to possible contexts (stimuli). For example, if Bill had told us this dream, we might wonder if he had had an incident with one of his male friends or with a girlfriend. We would be searching for triangular situations and for incidents in which sexuality played a role. We would wonder if something forbidden or dangerous, and sexual, had aroused Bill and created conflict.

SEARCHING FOR TRIGGERS

We might also propose that something might have stirred up the exhibitionistic or voyeuristic concerns in this dream. Perhaps something brought up Bill's brother and the whole issue of sibling relationships. There is also likely to be a trigger related to bodily disfigurement and damage, as well as precipitants involving themes of secrets, spies, and blackmailers. Finally, there must be a trigger that led to the images of fighting with the man.

All kinds of possibilities suggest themselves, so many that they become unfocused and therefore momentarily meaningless. However, it might be possible to think of some kind of trigger with multiple meanings that could unite some of these themes and therefore be a likely cause of their arousal. Perhaps there has been some form of sexual exposure or something sexually forbidden designed to evoke guilt, mistrust, and eventually hostility and anger. Then too it may well be that Bill observed something with forbidden sexual and hostile overtones, something that he perceived or fantasized as bodily dangerous. Whatever the experience or experiences, there seems to be a link to Bill's brother, Ken. Rather than speculate further, let us return to Bill.

Bill began again to mull over his dream. It was early in the morning, and while he was not entirely awake, he began to almost free associate. Being in bed with Sally and Rodger was an attractive thought. Rodger was his best friend, and Sally was Rodger's current girlfriend. Of late, Sally had been flirtatious with Bill. It dawned on Bill that Sally was being just a bit unfaithful to Rodger in flirting with him, Bill. Last night, when Bill and Millie (Bill's present girlfriend) had had dinner with Sally and Rodger, Sally's leg had brushed against Bill's more than once. He had wondered if she were making deliberate physical contact. In their conversation, Sally had also been quite seductive. Maybe, he thought, that's why she looked so dirty in the dream. And that could be why Bill had pulled away from her and left the bedroom in the dream. She was tempting all right, but Bill was not about to get involved in that kind of scene.

FLIRTATIOUSNESS: ONE TRIGGER

At this point, Bill is both the sender and the receiver of his dream message. While there are many ways we can react to our own dream expressions, we can see that Bill's particular response was to generate a series of surface messages or associations, each of which was linked in some vital way to an element in the dream. As noted, this response is not unlike the free associations of patients in psychoanalysis or insight psychotherapy. Contained in these further communications are additional encoded messages. Quite often, they contain at least one of the triggers for the dream. This is one advantage of this type of loose reaction to a dream experience, in contrast to efforts at direct decoding (intellectual readings) which are not only stultifying but also limit the range of associations so that the trigger is unlikely to emerge.

What, then, is the first trigger that Bill discovered? Clearly, it was Sally's flirtatious behavior at dinner on the night before the dream.

Once we have identified a particular trigger, we should immediately evaluate its manifest and latent implications. This trigger involves an evident sense of seductiveness and physical contact. It took place clandestinely and in the presence of two other people—Rodger and Millie. In its way, it tended to betray Rodger. To the extent that Bill participated and even unconsciously invited Sally's behavior, there would be an antecedent trigger as well.

In light of the implications of this particular stimulus, we can see immediately that through displacement, Bill has shifted the scene of action from the restaurant to his bedroom. Through a symbolic change (one that reverses the usual substitution of a more neutral image for one that is loaded with instinctual drive and other intense qualities), the flirtation is changed into a sexual liaison. This particular encoded image reflects both Bill's conscious and unconscious perceptions of Sally's seductiveness and his own responsive sexual fantasies. Here, through condensation, both perception and fantasy find a single communicative expression.

Sally's dirtiness is a symbolic representation of Bill's perception that she was betraying Rodger. The exhibitionistic quality of Sally's behavior is reflected in Bill's own nakedness and in the shade that is up in the bathroom. The pulling down of the shade appears to be a reaction to this seductiveness of a kind similar to Bill's originally pulling away from the bed.

Encoded here are perceptions of Sally's mixed attitudes toward Bill, and Bill's own conflicts regarding Sally. These concerns are highlighted toward the end of the dream where the theme of secrets appears and Bill is concerned with spies and blackmailers. Here, the unconsciously perceived discomfort in Sally and within Bill himself are represented once more through a mixture of encoded perception and fantasy. At the end of the dream, Bill repudiates a fresh illicit overture, and this leads to a fight. The dreamer seems to be asserting his decision to repudiate the perceived seductiveness in Sally and his aroused sexual longings and fantasies.

In all, this particular stimulus (Sally's seductiveness) has led to one level of trigger decoding that takes into account a large number, though not all, of the dream elements. In general, the interpretation of a dream is not complete until at least all of the major elements have been afforded one or more encoded meanings.

The inability to understand important aspects of this dream (e.g., the presence of Bill's brother Ken, the mole on Bill's arm, the spy—our understanding here seems especially incomplete—and Sally's menstruation) points to two main factors: first, the presence of relatively strong defenses (and therefore a high level of disguise), and second, the need to identify additional triggers for this dream. It is also possible that it is necessary to identify additional meanings contained in the original trigger, although it is important to not force efforts at decoding to the point where they are overstated.

For example, the mole could be thought of as Bill's castration-punishment for his sexual wishes toward Sally and his perception of some defect in Sally herself. Ken could be a homosexual stand-in for Sally, whom Bill unconsciously perceives as somewhat masculine and who also had stirred up defensive homosexual feelings within him. The further we get away from an immediate sense of clear encoded meaning in light of the trigger, the closer we are to direct decoding. If these are valid formulations, there should be additional support for them in subsequent messages.

AN ARGUMENT: A SECOND TRIGGER

Bill's thoughts went to a fight that he had had with Millie last night just before they had gone to bed together. Bill now thought of the fact that his brother Ken was divorced. Bill himself was becoming disillusioned with his relationship with Millie. The fight, which arose because Millie had pressed Bill in regard to his prior relationships with women and Bill had refused to answer, had been especially annoying.

We have here a second trigger for Bill's dream, a dispute between Bill and his girlfriend, her effort to pry secrets out of him, and his own loss of interest in Millie. The association to Ken's divorce is not a trigger but a related theme. It is an encoded message from Bill to himself: he now is thinking of leaving Millie, much as Ken had left his wife. The appearance of Ken in the dream is an encoded version of this particular fantasy-wish within Bill.

This particular trigger leads to an understanding of the dream as reflecting an encoded perception of Millie as wanting to provoke a rupture between herself and Bill, and through condensation, a fantasy in Bill that he would like to leave Millie. Here again we find condensation at work in producing a transversal message with a mixture of perception and fantasy. Bill's divided feelings toward Millie, as conveyed in the manifest dream, are expressed through displacement from Millie to Sally. Eventually, he pulls away; this element expresses again his fantasy of leaving Millie. Finally, the fight between Bill and the man is an encoded version of his fight with Millie.

Bill next thought of the fact that Millie was menstruating. This appears to validate the thesis that through displacement, Sally was on one level a stand-in for Millie, and that indeed, Bill had condensed a series of perceptions and fantasies regarding both women into many of these dream elements. There is also a further indication of the use of this particular mechanism in that Sally also stood for Ruth, Ken's wife. As we shall see later (from another trigger), she also represented a feminine, dirty, and damaged part of Bill himself.

For the moment, notice that the major representations (Sally as herself, Millie, and Ruth) have been identified in light of activated triggers rather than through direct decoding and speculation. They were guided by Bill's associations to the dream. They provided additional communicative segments which clarified the specific triggers and messages encoded within the dream.

It is evident that a single dream can contain an enormous number of encoded meanings and implications. The greater the number of significant triggers, the more intense the use of displacement and condensation, the more clever the use of symbols for multiple representations, the more complex the total conscious and unconscious messages. It is important to identify those triggers that are most pressing and those encoded responses that are most cogent. While decoding is a process that makes good use of creativity and imagination, it is nonetheless essential to attempt to stay as close as possible to the evident implications of a particular message and to introduce as little as possible of one's own fantasies as a decoder into the decoding process.

PAIN: A THIRD TRIGGER

As Bill ruminated on his dream, the mole on his arm reminded him of a rather black and ugly wart-like nevus (pigmented growth) on his leg which had been removed surgically several years earlier. He had been worried that it was cancerous but had been reassured that it was not. Of late, he had been having stomach pains. They had been rather intense during dinner that night. Bill now realized that he was once again concerned with having cancer or some other terrible illness inside of himself. The mole in the dream seemed grotesque. Maybe, he thought, he should see a doctor and have a checkup.

This train of thought produced a third trigger for Bill's dream: the stomach pains that Bill had experienced just before dinner and before falling alseep. If we were to specify the implications of this particular internal trigger, we would stress fears of illness and cancer and concerns with bodily damage.

The mole on Bill's arm is a displacement and externalization of his abdominal pains and his concern about an internal cancerous lesion. The uncertain image of Sally's menses and the blood on the sheets are poorly symbolized versions of Bill's fantasy that the cancer could destroy his insides or perhaps castrate him and turn him into a woman. It is of note that this particular image was the most dubious part of Bill's dream, a quality that suggests the presence of strong defenses. It seems evident, however, that Bill's defenses were only partially successful. They produced some measure of displacement, but the bodily anxieties were represented in frightening fashion.

Ken's perplexed state is a reflection of Bill's own sense of confusion and anxiety. Then too, the mole on his arm not only represents, through displacement, his concerns about a new lesion, but is also an encoded means through which Bill tries to reassure himself that, just as in the past the nevus had been successfully removed, so again in the present his symptoms could be taken care of by a physician.

This trigger explains the allusion to secrets as pertaining to something hurtful inside of Bill. The fight conveys Bill's protest against the possibility of being ill and damaged. It is also possible that in some way Bill's stomach pain was a type of self-punishment for Sally's seductiveness and his interest in her. The same symptom may also have been a response to his hostile thoughts toward Millie.

Since a later physical examination showed no physical basis for Bill's abdominal symptoms, we will treat them as a *somatic expression* of a psychological problem—a physical symptom that functions as an encoded message with latent contents.

Dreams and all encoded messages are not simply reflections of unconscious perceptions and fantasies. They are active efforts at coping and of trying to find solutions to intrapsychic and interpersonal problems and conflicts. An emotionally founded physical symptom is itself a form of encoded or unconscious expression. It is a type of communicative vehicle that entails some measure of pain for the sender and therefore reflects some degree of adaptive failure.

To this point, Bill's dream analysis reveals that through trigger decoding, Bill became more aware of his conflicted feelings toward Sally and her meaning for him. Understanding the dream also helped him to see his disillusionment with Millie and his thoughts of leaving her. With his conflicts more open and conscious he will be able to resolve them far more readily than if they had remained submerged.

Bill also became aware enough of his concerns about his physical health that he decided to see a doctor. He was even able to realize some of the psychological sources of his pain, and by resolving the related conflicts, he will be able to dispose of the symptoms. (They will no longer be necessary since the raw message itself will become conscious or be resolved and will therefore disappear.) At this point, Rodger's moustache will take on meaning and represent masculinity, strength, and physical intactness. This is another effort at reassurance of a kind that takes place directly or in encoded form in our dreams. Reassurance is an important function of these communications.

CONSCIOUS VERSUS UNCONSCIOUS FANTASIES ————

Bill had one final response to this dream as he mulled it over. Virtually always, there is a point at which our associations become thin and our interest wanders. Trigger decoding involves the pursuit of highly painful and conflicted messages; there is just so much the human mind can tolerate before invoking some rather gross defenses. We should just rest for a while at this point and think of other matters. Often we can return to the dream analysis later on with a freshness that permits further decoding and insight.

Bill's final response was puzzlement. He could not associate meaningfully to the secrets, the spy or blackmailer, his refusal of the offer, and the subsequent fight. While he had been able to link this particular part of the dream in some remote way to each of the three triggers he had already discovered, Bill sensed that something was missing. Unable to reach for it directly, he put the entire matter aside and waited for something to happen spontaneously.

This illustration can also help to establish the distinction between conscious and unconscious fantasies and conscious and unconscious perceptions. In regard to the former, it is important to realize that a *conscious* fantasy or daydream is usually an encoded (*unconscious*) message that has been evoked by a trigger. All too often, laypersons and therapists take these manifest fantasies and treat them as if they were direct expressions of the unconscious part of the mind. Nothing could be further from the truth. Whatever creates anxiety and symptoms must be encoded and therefore can be expressed only through encoded messages; whatever is admitted directly to consciousness may have a manifest meaning, but these are less of a threat than messages which require encoding. They do not directly illuminate transactions outside of awareness.

There are important differences between conscious and unconscious fantasies. The latter are, as we know, expressed in encoded fashion and tend to be far more threatening than the former. For example, Bill had a conscious fantasy that in some way Sally was attractive. He did not consciously imagine having intercourse with her, although this fantasy was clearly present in his dream. Similarly, Bill had not entertained directly the daydream of sharing a bed with Rodger and Sally, although this particular fantasy emerged directly in the manifest dream content. There are gradations of conscious and unconscious fantasy. Some are expressed consciously and directly (these usually have the least measure of threat), some emerge only with the lessening of defensiveness that takes place while dreaming, and some emerge only in encoded form (these, of course, tend to have the greatest degree of threat).

The same type of distinction applies to conscious and unconscious perceptiveness. While awake, Bill did notice that Sally had been seductive, although he had not perceived that she was playing a kind of dirty trick on Rodger; this latter he represented only in his dream. It was a particularly disturbing impression because on one level it also implied that he himself was involved in the betrayal. Similarly, Bill had not been aware of his own thoughts of leaving Millie, although these emerged quite strongly when he decoded his dream. These were highly disturbing impulses within himself, and they were quickly subjected to the encoding process.

In essence, then, manifest daydreams and fantasies may have meaning in themselves, although their most cogent implications involve their functions as disguised communications developed in response to triggers. There is no surface message that can spare us the use of trigger decoding when it is called for in our daily lives.

CHAPTER 13

HIDDEN TRIGGERS AND THEIR CONSEQUENCES

To return now to Bill and his dream, he next spent his morning at work. Bill then had lunch with Millie. He felt the need to tell her his dream and did so. He added some of his associations to the dream as well.

Millie's response came as something of a surprise to Bill. She reminded him that his father had a moustache and that there had been a long conversation at dinner about parents. But next, she rather cleverly said to him, "You know, I think you are trying to tell me something, and I'm really glad that you brought it up. I was pretty irritated with you last night at dinner. Maybe you thought I didn't hear you, but I did. It was really rotten of you to tell Rodger, after that spat he had with Sally, that he was welcome to come back to our apartment and sleep with us."

Bill was flabbergasted, and he was all the more so when he noted consciously for the first time that Millie had a mole on her left arm. Of course, he had completely forgotten his half-serious, half-joking remark to Rodger. He now remembered that Millie had become rather nasty not long after he had made his comment. Now he wondered why in the world he had said what he did. He was also incredulous that he had forgotten a wisecrack like that, especially in light of his dream.

HIDDEN MESSAGES

Millie had responded to Bill's dream with both conscious and unconscious decoding. She had rightly sensed that the dream contained important direct (manifest) and latent messages intended for her. She was readily able to see that Bill was unfaithful to her in the dream. She also knew that Ken was divorced. All of this was evidence of hidden messages that Millie had sensed for some time: she was fairly certain that Bill was distancing himself from her. For the moment she had no idea whether he would actually end their relationship. Still, she had been able to consciously decode part of Bill's dream in light of a trigger that had concerned her considerably—the ways in which she had been antagonizing Bill. Once she had provided him with this forgotten (repressed) trigger for his dream, both she and Bill were in a position to understand a number of its encoded messages. Most central was Bill's thoughts of other women.

In response to her realizations (her efforts at decoding), Millie at first mainly made use of some rather direct and manifest comments in order to express her displeasure with Bill. Because of the threat involved, she did not directly raise the question of his thoughts of leaving her. Instead, she went on to speak of how unhappy Ken had been since his divorce. This was her consciously encoded way of letting Bill know that she thought he would suffer if he broke up their relationship. Millie also had a few unkind things to say about Sally, warning Bill that she could be quite treacherous and bitchy. This was a partly direct and partly encoded way of responding to Bill's interest in Sally, and more broadly to his thoughts of other women.

In the course of their conversation, as the degree of disguise lessened on both sides, it was possible for Millie to confront Bill directly about their relationship and some of their recent problems. A process that had begun with the conscious and unconscious decoding of Bill's dream message ended with a direct effort to deal with what had become a troublesome and previously ignored aspect of his relationship with Millie.

Millie had another reaction to this dream. She felt disturbed about the presence of Rodger and Sally in bed with

Bill. She connected this element to Bill's invitation to Rodger but could take it no further. Later on, she remembered that Rodger had always seemed somewhat effeminate to her. Still, she had been unable to consciously identify the specific hidden message that lay beneath these impressions. It was here that lack of knowledge of the triggers of the dream and her own defenses came into play.

Nonetheless, it is possible to take these leads and to now decode a number of previously perplexing aspects of Bill's dream. Millie has provided us with some additional clues about certain dream elements, especially the image of the moustache. Bill's direct observation of the mole on Millie's arm also helps to illuminate previously repressed aspects of his dream.

First, Millie's disquieting experience appears to have been a response to the expression of hidden homosexual needs and fantasies in Bill. Without knowing it, she was attempting to bring these issues into his awareness since she had experienced an unconscious perception of Bill that, for reasons of her own, she was unable to allow access to direct consciousness. She had seen evidence of this kind of tendency within Bill in his invitation to Rodger, and in several of the other dream elements such as the fight with the spy or blackmailer. This problem was also reflected through the mole on Bill's arm, a dream element that showed most clearly his feminine identification with Millie.

Since he was somewhat sophisticated, Bill had a sense of this level of the dream's underlying meanings. He recognized that the dream must also have something to do with his relationship with his father, although he knew that the trigger for this particular undercurrent had not been identified. Bill was not an overt homosexual, although he knew something of his latent leanings in this direction. Had it been his disappointment in Millie that had shifted him toward homosexual fantasies? Had he seen something homosexual in Rodger, enough to have aroused his own needs? He now remembered the part of the dream in which Sally was bleeding and menstruating and thought that his image of his feminine self was apparently one that accentuated considerable bodily damage.

Hidden triggers.   Again we see that on deeper levels, the messages that we encode in dreams (for ourselves and others) are indeed highly charged and often perplexing. The dream is a means through which we work over and adapt to triggers that evoke in us reactions we cannot bear to deal with directly and manifestly. Sometimes, as in this instance, the threat is so great that we completely forget (repress) a particular trigger, or we fail to make an association that would prove to be the key to an underlying constellation of meanings that we wish to avoid at all costs. It is often necessary to engage in an extensive period of free association before arriving at these deepest and most anxiety-provoking raw images.

This sequence has also illustrated one of the ways in which we validate our impressions of the raw messages that underlie a manifest dream. In Bill's initial thoughts and associations, he had picked up tentative indications of an underlying homosexual fantasy and feminine identification. The associations prompted by Millie's reactions to the dream have elaborated in surprising and unexpected ways this particular theme. This development offers some confirmation for the initial formulation; it would be expected that once the trigger for this particular latent message is identified, it would further strengthen the sense of conviction that latent homosexuality is one of the underlying issues in this dream.

A FOURTH TRIGGER: THE PHONE CALL

Millie's reminder that there had been a discussion of parents at dinner led Bill to recall an unpleasant telephone conversation he had had with his mother earlier that day. In this way, he identified a fourth trigger for his dream. Since he had repressed this particular stimulus there was immediate reason to believe that it was especially pertinent to some of the dream's more threatening encoded raw messages. Bill's further associations lent considerable support to this thesis.

Thus Bill realized that he had been furious with his mother, who had been nagging and provocative on the telephone. His rage with her had undoubtedly influenced his attitude toward Millie, who could also at times be quite annoying. Bill tried to sort out the differences and similarities between Millie and his mother and to gain a better perspective on his relationship with both women. In addition, he quickly recognized that his rage toward his mother must have been the trigger for his own homosexual fantasies and longings; she was the source of considerable fear of and disillusionment with women.

This part of the dream now made considerably more sense to Bill and seemed to be falling into place. It led at last to a most convincing and unexpected bit of confirmation: a memory of an actual early homosexual experience with Ken that Bill had not recalled for some time. In this new light, it may well be that Bill's refusal to purchase the secrets in the dream was an attempt to repudiate his own homosexual wishes and the fight a means of asserting his masculinity in order to deny intense passive feminine longings. At the same time, the physical struggle may have gratified a number of unconscious aggressive homosexual fantasies. Through condensation (and displacement and symbolization), it had been possible for Bill to both deny and satisfy his homosexual wishes through a single dream element.

During their conversation, Bill's mother had mentioned plans to go away with his father to a small house that they owned at a lake resort. Bill thought little of this allusion, although it had set off, very much outside of his awareness, a number of memories that had been encoded in his dream. With some effort, he began to search for these recollections, using the manifest dream elements as his guide. He recalled sharing a bedroom with his parents as a child, although it was in another house at a different summer resort. Often, displacement operates several times over in helping to disguise a latent (raw) dream image. There may be displacements related to both present and past. The more active this mechanism, the more remote the derivative, the better the measure of disguise.

In this way, Bill became aware that his invitation to Rodger and his fantasies about Rodger and Sally had their fore-runners in experiences in his parents' bedroom. Involved here was a mixture of unconscious memory-perception and unconscious memory-fantasy. There were observations of the nudity of both of his parents, each stirring up threatening sexual perceptions and fantasies. There were observations of intercourse in which the main image accentuated the notion that his mother was in some way being damaged by his father.

There were many meanings to this interplay between the present and the past, although these will not be developed here. Mainly, we have seen how a repressed trigger, once discovered, can help to unravel especially disturbing encoded perceptions and fantasies, including their connection to still meaningful and threatening early childhood recollections.

The dream element of the mole on Bill's arm is a good example of a representation of an unconscious perception. That particular feature of Millie had never registered consciously in Bill's mind, although clearly he had made note of the mole in some way outside of his awareness. It required its presence in the dream and a fresh look at Millie to render this particular observation conscious. Further, quite unconsciously, Bill had made use of this particular unnoticed feature as a way of representing the presence of Millie in the dream. It is possible, then, that when there is an intense need for disguise, we make use of symbolic representations of which we are entirely unaware. Bill was deeply threatened by his conflicted feelings toward Millie, and by his thoughts of leaving her.

Once this train of thought had unfolded more openly and was connected to various elements of the dream, Bill was able to develop a fresh and relatively convincing insight into the final thread about the blackmailer. Bill had been involved in a number of questionable and probably illegal business practices. He had talked openly to Millie about these transactions. He now realized he harbored a deep concern that if he broke up with Millie, she might betray him. This, too, was a combination of fantasy and fear on the one hand and perception on the other. In a prior relationship, Millie had responded to the breakup with a vicious exposure of the man involved. By further decoding his dream, Bill had become aware of a number of serious conflicts and concerns that had virtually eluded his notice.

BILL'S ANALYTIC HOUR

After work, Bill went to his analytic hour. He had been in psychoanalysis for two years. As he walked toward the couch, he turned to Dr. Barker, his analyst, and commented, "I see there is no tape recorder on your desk today." (Dr. Barker, with Bill's permission, had recorded the previous session.) "No," replied the analyst, "I have enough to study for a while."

Once on the couch, Bill began to free associate. He spoke of his luncheon with Millie and of feeling annoyed with himself. Despite his misgivings about their relationship, he had very strong positive and loving feelings toward her. He was hesitant to give her up and regretted his insensitivity in inviting Rodger to share their bed. It was not like him to make a remark like that.

After lunch, largely because of his conversation with Millie, Bill had developed stomach cramps and had experienced a strong sense of anxiety. Why did he want to involve Rodger in his life to the point of sharing a bed with him? He didn't even like him all that much. It had spoiled things with Millie just at a time when he was trying to see if he could patch things up and make their relationship more meaningful and intimate.

At this point, Bill reported his dream. After running through some of his earlier associations, he suddenly realized that the bathroom in his dream reminded him of the lavatory in Dr. Barker's office. Rodger's moustache now brought to mind the country doctor who had taken care of his family when Bill was a young child. This led him to recall a painful episode from when he had been six or seven years old. The doctor had come to Bill's home and examined him for some reason. The experience was especially embarrassing because of the presence of not only his parents, but also his aunt and uncle, brother and sister, and two cousins who were all in the room at the time. In the midst of his examination, the physician had turned to Bill's mother and told her that her son's penis was unusually small. He also said something about some type of testicular problem. The incident was humiliating and embarrassing, and for years Bill had worried about being sterile. At the time, he had been furious with the doctor, although he had continued to see him for some years.

Next, Bill thought of a magazine article about a male psychotherapist who had seduced a female patient. A friend of Bill's had jokingly commented that some analysts are "AC-DC," both heterosexual and homosexual. Bill had always had mixed feelings toward his brother, though recently he had experienced a strong wish that they could be closer. Bill had tried a little, but his brother had put him off. He thought, "Maybe it's better that way. My brother is like a leech. He gets hold of people and never lets them go. He sucks them dry. He's into drugs a lot; he's very needy."

Bill's free associations went on: "The mole is a kind of defect. Blackmail is a vicious crime. All of us are criminals at heart. No one can be holier than his brethren." Secrets must have something to do with the analysis, but he hadn't felt like attacking the analyst of late.

CONSTELLATIONS OF ASSOCIATIONS

Since Dr. Barker offered an interpretation at this point in the session, it seems advisable to engage in our own efforts at decoding before hearing his particular formulation. In preparation, we might recognize the striking differences between Bill's associations to this dream when he was alone, when he was with Millie, and during his analytic hour. The three constellations are remarkably distinctive. This is perhaps most clearly seen in comparing Bill's private associations to those he imparted to Dr. Barker. The first group centered around Bill's relationships with Rodger, Sally, and Millie. They touched on his concerns about physical illness. In striking contrast, the associations to Dr. Barker seem to organize more around unexpected aspects of Bill's behavior with others, the leech-like attributes of his brother, and memories of the family doctor. Connections between the dream and Bill's relationship with Dr. Barker appeared for the first time in the presence of the analyst.

These impressions suggest two important points: first, that the presence of a particular receiver of an encoded message may greatly influence both the manifest and latent communications of the sender; and second, that, as noted before, the most threatening raw messages and the connecting associations can be so strongly defended against as to make it extremely difficult, if not impossible, for both the sender and receiver alike to detect the particular trend involved. At times of particular stress, it is important to persist in associating to dreams and in trying to decode them.

A FINAL TRIGGER: THE TAPE RECORDING

We will confine ourselves to a single trigger for this dream in Bill's relationship with Dr. Barker—the fifth and last stimulus that we will consider for this dream. Bill was still unaware that he had revealed it as he had entered his analyst's office. Though still repressed in Bill's mind, this particular trigger was perhaps the most significant day residue for the dream. It powerfully organized the dream and its associations into a highly coalescible set of meanings. The trigger was Dr. Barker's tape recording of Bill's session.

Until now, we have been working mainly from manifest messages back to the trigger, doing so by undoing the dreamer's use of displacement, condensation, and symbolization. Here, as our final exercise in the trigger decoding of this dream, we will analyze the manifest and latent implications of the trigger first, and thereby derive several raw but unconscious perceptions of Dr. Barker that required encoding because of their dangerous qualities. This analysis of the implications of the stimulus will also enable us to identify possible anxiety-inducing fantasies that it might have evoked in Bill and which would also have appeared in encoded fashion in his dream.

What, then, are the conscious and unconscious qualities of an action by an analyst in the form of tape recording a session with a patient? One of the best ways to characterize a trigger is to place oneself in the receiver's place (the use of trial identification and empathy). You then ask yourself, "How would I feel if my analyst, whatever his explanation, tape recorded one of my sessions? Previously, my analysis has been private and confidential. Now it is being put on tape."

In actuality, Dr. Barker had explained that he thought it would be helpful if he took some time to analyze one of his sessions with Bill. On that basis, Bill had agreed. He had accepted Dr. Barker's manifest message at face value and had not engaged in any effort at conscious decoding (when it comes to the analyst's interventions, patients—and therapists—seldom do).

In general, a tape recording leads a patient to feel on some level manipulated and used, despite the additional (usually conscious) satisfaction that the analyst is deeply interested and exerting a special effort on one's behalf. Bill's privacy was being invaded, and he would likely have a sense of exposure and endangerment. He might worry that the tape would be presented to a supervisor, at a teaching conference, or—who knows?—at a public forum. Whatever the constructive intentions, taping conveys a sense of invasion, of being devoured and seduced, and of having one's words captured and possessed forever. It would obliterate the usual boundaries between Bill and his analyst. In a way, Bill might also feel merged and one with his analyst, never to be separated from him, in some sense a part of him.

Almost always, the receiver of a powerful message will register its implications unconsciously. Some sophisticated listeners will consciously identify a number of its meanings; others maintain a surface naiveté despite multiple unconscious registrations. In this situation, Bill tended consciously to trust his analyst (though with some wariness) and not to question his interventions and proposals. He was preoccupied with some problems at work and with his relationship with Millie and gave virtually no conscious thought to the fact that he had gone through a recorded session. It remains now for us to see how Bill had *unconsciously* experienced this particular trigger and how his raw perceptions (and reactive fantasies) were transformed into his manifest dream.

We might begin with Bill's behavior at dinner the night before. He had been abusive with his girlfriend and had invited a third party (Rodger) to join them in bed. In light of the trigger that Bill was working over at the time, we can now understand that his inexplicable behaviors were actually conscious messages that contained encoded unconscious perceptions of Dr. Barker's decision to tape record the session. Long before Bill had had his dream, his actions with others had been strongly and unconsciously influenced by his analyst's intervention.

The implications of the tape recording had been incorporated unconsciously by Bill. They created tension in him and his tension then influenced his interactions with others. These interactions were an attempt to cope with the disturbance caused by his analyst, largely through displacement in that Bill was as yet not consciously aware of the problem. At the same time, Bill's behaviors could be seen as a way of expressing and communicating his own unconscious reading of the encoded messages from his therapist. Seemingly irrational actions of this kind, then, are motivated by triggers that create need systems within the receiver and are therefore both a responsive mode of adaptation and a mode of communication (an effort to resolve the problem and to represent its existence as well).

Bill's incorporated unconscious perception was that Dr. Barker had mistreated and abused his patient. This led unconsciously to Bill's mistreatment and abuse of Millie (through displacement and an identification with the analyst). In addition, by introducing the tape recording into the session, it was as if Dr. Barker had invited not only a machine as a third party to treatment, but a potential audience as well. Entirely without being aware of it, Bill's invitation to Rodger to join him in bed with Millie was an encoded version of an unconsciously perceived meaning inherent to the trigger of Dr. Barker's introduction of the tape recorder.

To complete the analysis of this particular theme, we can see now that Dr. Barker's tape recording was experienced as a seduction and as the introduction of an intruder. Genetically, this had a meaning comparable to the invitation in his childhood reflected in Bill's parents' decision to allow him to share their bedroom. While it may appear that it is Bill rather than his analyst who is introducing the sexual qualities into the tape recording experience, psychotherapy research has actually shown that behaviors of this kind by analysts are typically motivated by unconscious and unresolved pathological sexual fantasies of the very kind that this patient had perceived unconsciously. There is therefore a strong mixture of unconscious perception and unconscious fantasy in these encoded expressions.

Bill's memory of the childhood physical examination is also connected to this trigger. The memory exquisitely captures a number of Bill's current perceptions and fantasies, many of them related to the feeling that he was being exposed sexually in his therapy only to be seen as terribly inadequate. (Note the remarkable use of concerns for representability—the use of a memory as part of a logical conscious narrative as well as a means of conveying critical encoded messages.) At the same time, through condensation (and displacement and symbolism) these associations represent Bill's unconscious perception of his analyst as inadequate sexually and otherwise, as revealed by his need to tape record the session. After all, the argument would go, there is no reason why a competent analyst would have to study a tape recording of a session in order to understand his patient; he should be able to understand the patient in the course of his daily work. In a sense, then, there is considerable validity to Bill's communicated unconscious perception of some revealed inadequacy in his therapist.

The seductive and sexual qualities of the tape recording are strongly tinged with homosexual meanings as well. These help to account for the evidence of Bill's homosexual fantasies, which were combined through condensation with unconscious perceptions of homosexual needs in his therapist. The image of the damaged woman then alludes on one level to Bill's feeling that he was being placed in a passive and abused position, and on another to his perception of his analyst as ineffectual and as trying to compensate for some inner sense of damage of his own.

To point out some further aspects of Bill's dream and associations: Sally's dirtiness is Bill's unconscious perception of Dr. Barker doing something inappropriate and soiling. His behavior resembles the hurtful actions of Bill's father, and this link accounts for the moustache that Rodger was sporting. Bill at first felt stimulated and gratified by his analyst's request, but then had second thoughts. Thus, in the dream he is at first involved in a ménage à trois but then pulls away. Here, he offers a model to the analyst to correct the situation and to forgo further tapings.

The nakedness, of course, alludes to Bill's feeling that he was being exposed and to the problems that the analyst exposed Bill to through his request. The homosexually seductive aspects are represented in encoded form through the appearance of Bill's brother, Ken, who had once seduced Bill and who himself tended to be rather effeminate. The theme of Ken's separation from his wife involves unconscious thoughts within Bill that maybe he would terminate his analysis because of his negative perceptions of Dr. Barker.

The bathroom provides a specific link between the scene of the dream and Dr. Barker's office, thereby revealing the operation of displacement and the key to the latent dream images. The uncovered bathroom window repeats the theme of Bill's and Dr. Barker's exposure, and strikingly, Bill once again attempts to rectify the situation by pulling down the shade.

Finally, the spy or blackmailer—the most mysterious and obscure part of the dream—is a representation of Dr. Barker. It is here that Bill reveals in derivative fashion his feelings of exploitation and of being spied upon and open to blackmail. He reveals, too, his unconscious (that is, unregistered) objections to the tape recording and in his dream fights back in a way he could not during his session. All too often we react consciously in a highly submissive manner to hurtful triggers only to express our violent protest through a dream or a displaced behavior. This type of reaction is especially common when it is triggered by unconscious perceptions of another person that are deeply disturbing. Bill's unconscious view of his analyst as exploitative, intrusive, and, especially, as dishonest, created such painful realizations and conflict that he needed to erect massive defenses against their conscious registration.

Although there are many other ramifications of this network of communications—dream, behaviors, and associations —we will consider but one: another encoded and condensed meaning of the presence of Ken in this dream. This particular set of meanings emerged in Bill's associations to the presence of his brother in the dream. As the reader may recall, these touched upon Ken's greediness, leech-like qualities, and penchant for drugs. It is here through a doubly displaced encoded message that Bill represented his most painful unconscious perceptions of these very qualities in his analyst. Whatever these attributes had to do with Bill himself (and they did), they were for the moment very soundly perceptive of his analyst.

THE ANALYST'S INTERPRETATION

To finish our story, Dr. Barker proved capable of recognizing several hidden messages in Bill's communications. He pointed out to his patient that he had started the session by referring to the absence of the tape recorder. He proposed that there were many indications that Bill was reacting to the recording of his previous hour. He seemed to be experiencing it, in light of his dream, as the creation of a sexual threesome which both attracted and repulsed him. The introduction of a tape recorder had led Bill to see him—Dr. Barker—as a dirty, bloody, damaged woman who was about to expose and humiliate him as had his mother and a physician in the past. The tape recording was also seen as sexually seductive and a reflection of homosexual needs; it was also a vehicle for blackmail and spying. The doctor suggested that Bill was infuriated by all of this. He wanted it not to have occurred, expressing the wish in his dream by walking away from the threesome, pulling down the shade, and fighting the blackmailer. By all indications, then, Bill felt that the tape recording of his session was a highly destructive and inappropriate act, addictive and devouring, that the tape should be destroyed, and his sessions never be recorded again. Dr. Barker agreed, and indicated that he would carry out Bill's wishes in this regard.

Bill laughed. "You know," he said, "It just occurred to me that my brother is in the record business. He's been involved in making a number of bootleg records of late. I had warned him the other day that he was in danger of being caught and sent to jail. I had told him that it was a dishonest and corrupt way to earn a living and that it was a sign that he had bankrupted himself intellectually. I strongly advised him to desist before it was too late."

Here, of course, we have an elaborate encoded validation of Dr. Barker's interpretation, which itself had been based on a very effective form of trigger decoding. Fortunately for Bill, Dr. Barker was not the kind of analyst who simply engaged in direct decoding and who would have attributed this dream to Bill's own homosexual conflicts and early primal scene experiences, without taking into account any of the stimuli within the therapeutic interaction. Both patient and analyst were rewarded by several additional encoded messages which led to further insights into the situation on both the direct and derivative levels, thereby clarifying the impact of the tape recording on Bill, much of it quite outside of his awareness.

We have been able to observe someone who began his day with a strongly encoded, multiple-meaning message. Had he functioned differently, Bill might have started off by becoming preoccupied by the fact that his analytic session had been tape recorded and with a feeling that something was amiss. He might then have worked over the implications of the trigger and attempted to detect his own unconscious reactions to the stimulus. In real life, trigger decoding can begin at either end: with an analysis of the trigger itself or with a study of a responsive encoded message. In either case, the goal is the detection of underlying raw messages that are outside of awareness and which, nonetheless, exert considerable influence over the individual and his or her behaviors. Through this kind of effort, Bill was able to clarify a number of conflicts, his specific problem with Millie, aspects of his relationship with his mother (past and present), the sources of several symptoms, and a number of unresolved issues in his relationship with his analyst. Without the use of trigger decoding, none of this would have been feasible. Bill might have been led into a destructive ménage à trois or into a dishonest business deal that could have eventuated in a jail sentence. It is the inordinate power of unconscious perceptions and fantasies and of the conflicts that they evoke to influence our daily lives that makes trigger decoding such a valuable resource.

PART III
MEANING AND NONMEANING, TRUTH AND LIE

CHAPTER 14
STYLES OF COMMUNICATION

To this point, we have paid virtually no attention to how people differ in sending and receiving messages, including their responses to highly meaningful triggers. We have focused on positive communication and have not considered at all the possibility of noncommunication—the absence or destruction of meaning (and, with it, meaningful relatedness).

In general, psychoanalysts and others interested in communication and dynamic understanding assume the constant presence of meaning within their patients and others. In the absence of seemingly meaningful or interpretable material, they propose the existence of defenses or resistances. They believe that meaning is present but that the patient fears its realization and therefore closes it off. With the removal of the defense, they believe, the meaning will emerge.

Psychoanalysts sometimes have been described as individuals who can assign meaning to absolutely anything in the world. They are indeed deeply invested in assigning meaning; in general, the idea that there could be individuals who prefer to seal off or destroy meaning has simply not dawned on them. Two British psychoanalysts, Masud Khan (1973) and Wilfred Bion (1977), have proved to be the exceptions to this trend and have proposed this very possibility. But very little attention has otherwise been paid to these problems. (In fact, their existence has not been registered.)

Part of the difficulty arises from the limitations of most present-day psychoanalytic decoding measures. As noted, these virtually always involve the use of self-evident inferences and the direct decoding of postulated intrapsychic and genetic (childhood-related) stirrings within the patient. Since virtually every communicative expression can be assigned an isolated meaning of this kind, the presence of nonmeaning is not at issue.

However, matters are considerably different when trigger decoding is the basic approach to an understanding of unconscious communication. Through the identification of emotionally charged triggers, we can determine whether an individual responds actively and meaningfully or with denial of impact and a response essentially devoid of activated meaning. While there are, of course, shadings in intensity in people's experience of stimuli, it nonetheless can be safely stated that there exist a wide variety of universally meaningful emotional stimuli. It is therefore possible to distinguish perceptive from obliterating responses.

THE TRUTH SENDER AND RECEIVER

The issue then becomes whether a particular receiver of a charged message responds with meaningful manifest and especially encoded expressions. We can identify those individuals who respond to emotionally laden triggers through meaningful communicated expressions of their own. Because they are working over in meaningful fashion an actual source of disturbance, we can term them *truth senders*. The term implies that these individuals acknowledge on some level the existence of a disturbing trigger and work it over (adapt to it) in meaningful fashion. They are dealing, then, with the true (interactional-intrapsychic) source of an emotional problem rather than avoiding or falsifying it.

In practical communicative terms, we can develop a straightforward empirical definition of the truth sender. He or she is an individual who directly or in thinly encoded fashion represents a disturbing trigger in passing and then provides a series of encoded communicative responses that are quite diverse and which coalesce meaningfully around the implications of the trigger at hand. Thus, the ideal hallmark of the truth sender is a brief but direct representation of a disruptive trigger and a diversely meaningful encoded communicative response.

As for *truth receivers*, they are individuals who are open to the valid meanings in the messages of others. They can be identified by their ability to process consciously the most important meanings of messages received. However, in addition—and this is essential to the definition—they are able to respond with an encoded message of their own which, upon analysis, reveals a definitive extension of the implications of the received message. These individuals therefore acknowledge meaningful messages on two levels: consciously and directly, and unconsciously through encoded responses. Further, they meaningfully work over the received implications of messages in a fashion that reflects sound coping and extensions of understanding.

THE LIE SENDER AND RECEIVER

In contrast, the *lie* or *lie-barrier sender* is an individual who fails to provide this type of communicative complex. He or she fails to mention a critical trigger, or having done so, does not proceed to generate a meaningful derivative response. The communicative material may be quite fragmented, but whatever form it takes, there is a destruction of one or more elements of a complete communicative network (a represented trigger and coalescible derivative reaction).

Lie senders therefore wish *not* to deal with disturbing triggers and prefer instead to seal off their impact and to disregard their meanings and implications. Quite unconsciously, they either totally wall off the truth of a generated disturbance (create a lie-barrier system) or substitute lies or fictions in its place. *Lie receivers* obliterate and destroy the meanings of incoming messages. They show no direct sign of understanding, and they do not produce encoded elaborations of the implications of messages received. They maintain an attitude of nonmeaning on both levels.

STYLES OF UNCONSCIOUS COMMUNICATION ⸻⸻

This delineation of senders and receivers is based on the manner in which a given person responds consciously and especially unconsciously to emotionally charged triggers. The four communicative styles identified to this point—truth senders and receivers, and lie senders and receivers—find their clearest distinction in the presence or absence of a meaningfully encoded unconscious response to these emotional stimuli. The delineation is based on the proposition that the most essential truths of an emotionally charged situation are derived from the nature of the stimulus, the unconscious communicative interaction between the sender and the receiver, and the conscious and unconscious intrapsychic and interpersonal dynamics and stirrings aroused in both by their exchange of messages.

Clearly, this is a specific definition of truth that has been fashioned mainly to account for the core factors in emotional disturbances, although it may be applied more broadly to all emotionally charged human situations. The definition focuses on the core unconscious determinants of emotional disturbance and the issue of whether a particular person chooses to deal actively and meaningfully with them or to obliterate and avoid their ramifications.

Certainly, there are other truths that touch upon emotional disturbance. There are familial factors, the influence of society and culture, and a variety of surface considerations. Nonetheless, emotional illness has as one of its most critical determinants influences outside of the awareness of the individual involved (unconscious perceptions and fantasies). Further, it has been determined empirically that the manner in which a given person copes with these unconscious images and messages is an extremely useful approach to understanding communicative propensities, the nature of emotional disturbances, and human psychology in general.

It is to be stressed, then, that we are dealing here with *unconscious* communicative tendencies and not at all with the surface of human interchanges. This particular classification does not rely on people's conscious use of truth or falsifications but on an unconscious tendency that exists beyond the deliberate control of the sender or receiver. It is therefore a trend that can be identified only through an analysis of triggers and the responses to them. As can be seen, then, we are not in any way dealing with the morality of lying or telling the truth, or with issues of truth and falseness in any pejorative sense. We are considering two basic styles of communication: one that embraces and works over the truth of the core situation and the other that fails to do so.

DETERMINANTS OF COMMUNICATIVE STYLES

The two fundamental human communicative styles have very distinctive assets and liabilities. They seem to be on a continuum, with a group of persons in the middle who appear to be either well-defended truth tellers or less rigid unconscious liars. There is as well some initial evidence that each of these styles develop very early in life, based on an interaction between innate givens, the nature of parental care, the communicative styles of the parents, and life events. In general, once established, these communicative tendencies are relatively stable and quite difficult to modify.

QUIET COMMUNICATION AND DUMPING

One final variable influences these expressive tendencies. It involves the extent to which communication is effected through well-modulated words and language, accompanied by suitable affects, or through pressure behaviors—forms of action and discharge (even when words are used) that involve a great deal of dumping of the sender's own inner tensions and conflicts into the receiver. We may term the first style *quiet communication*, a type of message sending that is generally recognized. On the other hand, the second style, *dumping*, has received attention in some psychoanalytic circles but has been neglected in others. Because this particular dimension of communication has a great influence on the nature of expressed messages and their effects on the sender and receiver, it will be afforded special attention. There are, as we will see, truth dumpers and lie dumpers (senders), and truthful but dumping receivers and lying but dumping receivers.

The classification that we will use, then, does not concern itself with surface truths and lies. A manifestly truthful statement can be used to falsify a perception or a reaction to an emotional trigger. A deliberate, conscious lie can similarly falsify a stimulus or represent an *unconsciously* truthful response. The discovery of adaptive sequences that begin with triggers and lead to encoded reactions has permitted us to make this particular classification. As we will see, many relationships fraught with communicative confusion can be improved or at least understood with the recognition that the individuals involved are utilizing distinctly different modes of communicative expression.

CHAPTER 15

TRUTH SENDERS AND TRUTH RECEIVERS

Once moral influence and blind idealization are set aside, it can be readily acknowledged that there are some truths that are at best mixed blessings. Certain truths offer us something constructive without causing pain; other truths are either devastatingly destructive or constructive only in the face of an accompanying measure of pain and suffering. These qualities must be tolerated and mastered so that the truths involved can be integrated into a fresh level of insight and sound functioning.

For example, those truths that led to a better understanding of the universe, of the human body and the cure of its ills, and most forms of scientific knowledge are relatively painless truths with practical meanings and uses that are quickly embraced by most. On the other hand, the realization of those truths that are related to emotional disturbance are so personally threatening as to cause considerable defensiveness and avoidance. They are painful truths whose mastery leads to a higher level of functioning and coping than before, and yet whose tolerance and working through ask a great deal of the individuals involved. To recognize and work over our utter helplessness in the face of death; the inevitable pain of separation from loved ones (from our mothers on); perceptions of unconscious wishes in loved ones to abuse, exploit, and even murder us; and the conscious experience of our own primitive, violent, and reckless sexual fantasies (of incest, dismemberment, cannibalism, corruption, and the like) involve the experience of truths difficult to tolerate and even more difficult to digest and master. Yet these are the truths that underlie emotional dysfunction, the small or large measure of inner disturbance that exists in all of us.

THE CHOICE TO FLEE OR FIGHT

Because the truths involved are horrendous, we quite naturally erect defenses such as flight, denial, repression, and the like against their open expression. The moment of truth, so to speak, arrives only when a pivotal reality experience presses us, often in the name of psychic survival, to face some of these highly disturbing inner or outer actualities. It is at this type of juncture that our communicative coping capacities are mobilized quite automatically, and the unconscious choice is made either to represent in some meaningful form the difficult truths involved in order to adapt through understanding (truth telling) or to find some means of obliterating or falsifying the actualities of the situation (lying).

There is evidence now that our instincts and inborn tendencies initially make liars (in this sense) of us all. On a psychobiological level, when it comes to emotionally threatening triggers, the natural propensity is to opt for flight rather than fight. We require special capacities and tolerance to do otherwise. There are signs, then, that the truth receiver and truth sender are individuals who have developed a unique set of abilities to tolerate and work over emotionally charged truths. Lie receivers or lie senders have remained fixated at a level commensurate with our far more primitive endowments.

To this point, all of the senders we have studied were truth senders. In particular, Betty, even though she was a child, meaningfully represented important truths that had impinged upon her in connection with her parents' divorce. Bill was coping with a series of painful triggers, each of which he eventually represented and worked over (rather than obliterating). One more brief example of a truth sender-truth receiver (the two need not always go together) will form a basis for further discussion of this particular communicative style.

A KNIGHT TO THE RESCUE ————————————————————————

Mrs. Baker—Peggy—was a married woman in her late twenties. She was two months pregnant when she began to bleed spottily. When cramps developed and medication failed, she was hospitalized. That afternoon she had a spontaneous abortion.

Later that day, her husband, George, visited her. On his way to her hospital room, he noticed a floral arrangement with a knight in armor as decoration. Before he knew it, he was having a daydream of living in King Arthur's era.

A beautiful woman was incarcerated in a castle dungeon. There was a raging storm, and the river near the castle was overflowing. The dungeon was being flooded. The damsel cried out hysterically, hoping to be rescued from drowning. Boldly, George, knight in shining armor, entered the castle, slew the damsel's jailers, and set the beautiful maiden free.

The trigger for this daydream is self-evident. A miscarriage is a major traumatic stimulus for all concerned. It is the kind of emotional disturbance that is acute and that demands adaptation. Among George's coping efforts was this conscious fantasy. Within its confines lies a sequence of hidden messages that George has sent to himself in an effort to understand and work over what has happened. If he told the fantasy to his wife, Peggy, it would be part of his way of letting her know, through disguised communication, some of his feelings, perceptions, and conscious and unconscious (encoded) fantasies. Much of her response would then depend on how Peggy received George's messages and what portion was subjected to conscious decoding and what portion remained unconsciously perceived though not consciously registered.

We will not concern ourselves with George's associations to this fantasy. We are already in a position to decode some of its hidden meanings in light of the more universal implications of Peggy's miscarriage (to which, in real life, it would be necessary to add the very specific meanings of this event for both George and his wife).

We will begin by attempting to identify the manifest and latent implications of a miscarriage. On the surface, it involves the loss of a fetus and the inability of a pregnant woman to sustain a pregnancy. On deeper levels, in mixtures of perception and fantasy, it would evoke images of death, murder, and loss of a bodily part; bleeding, hemorrhage, and loss of control; and images related to an incapacity to hold and contain, implying poor mothering and caring. A miscarriage would evoke feelings of loss, rejection, and damage; guilt in having created and lost or destroyed a fetus; images of internal devastation; and fears of retaliation and vengeance on the part of the aborted fetus. For George, in particular, there would also be concerns about having helped to create a defective fetus, fears that in some way his having had relations with his wife not long before the miscarriage might have damaged her and the growing child, and, more broadly, worries that in some fashion he himself had contributed to the damage done to his wife and to the loss of the unborn child.

Although virtually everyone will respond to an enormously charged trigger with a small measure of meaning and representation, only a certain percentage (an intelligent initial guess runs somewhere between thirty and fifty percent) will respond with a large measure of the truths involved.

Because George was on his way to visit his wife soon after her miscarriage, there is strong reason to propose that this event was the precipitant for his daydream. Just before he had been distracted by the flowers, he had thought again about the miscarriage and his sense of upset for his wife, the fetus, and himself.

Momentarily, his daydream had removed him from these concerns. On the manifest level, there is no direct allusion to the trigger (i.e., this is not a direct and conscious fantasy about the miscarriage). It seems likely, then, that the first function of this daydream was to remove George from the immediate pain of the trigger and, in all likelihood, to enable him to work over his responsive disturbance through encoded messages. This effort is immediately represented and supported by George's transposition into the distant past. It is substantiated, too, by the momentary pleasure that George experienced in weaving his rescue fantasy.

LIGHT IN THE DUNGEON

It remains for us (and for George) to attempt to decode this particular fantasy-message in light of its trigger. In George's daydream, he is a knight in armor, and there is a damsel in a dungeon who is about to be drowned in a flood of water. In a miscarriage, a fetus enclosed in a womb is damaged and eventually destroyed and extruded. The drowning damsel, then, seems to be a creatively encoded, relatively detoxified (nonthreatening) image of the endangered fetus. As such, it is probably the best representation of Peggy's pregnancy.

Next, we can readily infer (decode) that it was George's unconscious wish that he could have prevented the miscarriage (represented here by rescuing the maiden). One of the main functions of the daydream, then, is to express this wish in encoded form. It has been disguised perhaps because, first, George did not want to face his criticisms of his wife's obstetrician, whom he felt might have acted more wisely and prevented the abortion. Secondly, and more important, the daydream was disguised as a defense against feelings within George that his wife was in some way responsible for the loss of their child. Finally, of course, this part of George's fantasy was motivated by his need to believe that he himself had in no way contributed to the loss of the fetus, a painful raw message (self-accusation) with which George was struggling and over which he felt considerable guilt.

We can see already that George had meaningfully represented in encoded fashion the miscarriage itself; a number of unconscious perceptions of his wife, her obstetrician, and himself in connection with this experience; and several fantasied responses of his own to the situation. Thus George had indeed meaningfully portrayed the situation and had chosen to deal through encoded messages with its actual implications. George was therefore functioning as a truth sender, and if he were able to decode and work over any part of these encoded messages, he would be seen as a truth receiver as well.

To reinforce this impression, let us analyze only one other aspect of this complex daydream: that George slays the damsel's jailers. Here, through the use of condensation, displacement, and symbolic representation, George is able in highly disguised and detoxified form to represent his fantasy-perception that the miscarriage is a form of murder. Included here is George's unconscious fantasy that his wife (the keeper of the fetus) had killed the budding child, that the obstetrician (also the guardian of the pregnancy) had done so, and/or that he himself was responsible. The single image condenses all three beliefs into one expression. And yet, on still another level, the same image represents simultaneously through further condensation George's violent feelings about the miscarriage as directed toward each of these three individuals.

We can see that George was dealing with extremely violent and destructive images. He could not experience them directly without being driven crazy. By making use of a highly creative encoding process, George was able simultaneously to defend himself against these terrible realizations and to express their contents so that their meaning would become available to him if he made efforts at conscious decoding (i.e., became a truth receiver). Had he done so, he would then have had an opportunity to work over at a seemingly safe distance some of his more disturbing and conflicted responses to the miscarriage. It is far more effective to encode a message of murderous violence and then to observe that message at a distance than to feel immediately, murderously violent and to lose control.

The working over of a traumatic trigger through encoded messages is highly adaptive indeed. Through proper decoding, the entire experience would place George in a position where he would better understand his perceptions and fantasies of the situation and his reactions to it as well. With such insight, he would be able to cope in a way that would preclude, for example, a sudden and inexplicable attack on his wife, an outburst of irrational hostility toward her obstetrician, or even a guilt-ridden suicide attempt of his own. These are the adaptive advantages that accrue to the truth sender and truth receiver—although clearly at rather painful cost.

THE SEARCH FOR TRUTH

In order to function within a truth system (a represented trigger and a meaningful encoded response), an individual must have a capacity to tolerate pain, to delay immediate responsive action (which would tend to be designed to discharge the situation, to extrude its meanings), and to surrender a notable measure of near-automatic defensiveness in order to permit and tolerate expressions of the truth of the incident. The individual must also manage the impulse directed toward immediate defensiveness and forgo the almost automatic search for immediate relief.

RELATING MEANINGFULLY WITH OTHERS

On a different level, the truth sender and receiver relates meaningfully to others. Relationships are open communicatively and filled with affect and meaning on both the surface and in the depths. The truthful relationship tends to be *commensal* (providing equal caring satisfactions for both parties), or a form of *healthy symbiosis* (providing a major source of care for one person, the *symbiotic recipient*, while providing a significantly less definitive sense of satisfaction for the other, the *symbiotic donor*). It is these two forms of basic relatedness that are most healthy and which promote growth and individuation as well as an appropriate measure of dependency in the members of relationship dyads. In this way, style of communication is a major determinant and reflection of how we relate to others.

The truth sender, then, meaningfully encodes and represents the sources of his or her distress as well as his or her responses. These messages are a mixture of valid encoded perception and fantasy. They contain many different levels of indirect response and serve a number of distinct purposes. These involve exquisite perceptions of the nature of the issues, fantasied reactions, evoked early memories (genetics), a variety of hopes and expectations, attempts at cure and harm, as well as a number of different efforts at coping. These are therefore rich in potentially adaptive resources despite the pain of the realizations involved.

ASSETS AND LIABILITIES

To summarize, the assets of truth receiving and sending are those that accrue from a genuine working over of a disturbing trigger. The individual so inclined is in a position to adapt to a difficult situation in a manner that least penalizes the individuals involved and offers the greatest promise of future successful adaptations, as well as personal growth and relative autonomy. Truth receiving and sending are means of expression and communication that foster healthy forms of relatedness with many satisfactions for all concerned. Indeed, they are the only basis through which we can genuinely grow and mature emotionally and psychologically.

As for liabilities, truth receivers and senders, in response to a traumatic trigger, will inevitably experience a period of seemingly catastrophic chaos. They will be confronted with extremely painful realizations relating to themselves and others. Momentary disturbance is inevitable and, at times, the anxiety and depression may be all but unbearable. Thus, working with the truth produces a large measure of turmoil and entails a significant risk, a danger that can be approached only with a strong measure of faith in one's own ultimate coping capacities. The uncertainty of ultimate resolution and of holding up under the pressures of truthful realizations are often difficult to endure.

It is to be stressed, then, that the truth system is but one means of coping. It does indeed have its advantages and disadvantages. It is a capacity that requires considerable maturity, much of it undoubtedly derived from early experiences with a mothering figure capable of tolerating both the expression of emotional truths herself and their expression in her child. Coping through truth is part of a complex mode of adaptation to the unconscious dimension of an emotionally charged situation.

Interchanges between two truth senders and receivers are, as a rule, quite meaningful and adaptive. This type of relationship usually involves a manifest use of the truth, though its essential characteristic is an interchange of meaningful encoded messages that is ultimately subjected to conscious decoding and manifest realization. There is an opportunity for both parties to resolve both interpersonal issues and those that are intrapsychic in a manner unavailable in the presence of obliteration. While it is possible for a truth obliterator to weave a magnificent piece of fiction designed almost entirely to falsify a disturbing life situation, there may well be a particular kind of richness to truth-based creations. However, it is quite clear that scientific discovery and progress, as well as personal growth, can take place in genuine and lasting form only by representing painful unconscious but truthful implications.

CHAPTER 16

LIE SENDERS AND LIE RECEIVERS

At moments of sobering thought, it is not especially surprising to find that lies, conscious and unconscious, are among our most often used means of protection in emotionally charged situations. In part, the scientific study of lies (fictions) and lie-barrier defensive formations has been delayed because of the penumbra of meanings that surround the term: dishonesty, evil and badness, forbidden and morally wrong. And yet, psychoanalysts have shown that often that which is most forbidden is most tempting. Although it is true that there is something inherently destructive in a lie, we should not underestimate its strange and compelling power to serve and protect us. The lie system, then, has its own value and liabilities and must be understood on its own terms.

A sense of the adaptive value of lies may be gleaned from the concept of the white lie: a permissible falsehood offered to another person to spare him or her pain or to ease his or her discomfort. When the truth is too brutal, lies are often an acceptable substitute.

As we know, a conscious lie is a deliberate or unwitting, but evident, falsification of consensually validated reality. Most often, the term *lie* implies deliberate misrepresentation; the term *error* usually implies a genuine mistake or an unintended misconception.

A manifest lie alters reality to suit the liar's needs. The liar sends messages that cannot be trusted and that tend to be distorted and unpredictable. The receiver is often confused and uncertain in the presence of a liar and must undertake special forms of validation in response to lies. When the existence of the lie is not immediately apparent, it is detected by criteria related to reality. Its discovery significantly alters the relationship between sender and receiver.

In general, the deliberate liar shows an intolerance for reality and a need for pathological omnipotence. He or she is unable to postpone the gratification of his or her usually inordinate needs. He or she is likely as well to be an unconscious liar (a type to be more fully defined below). Nonetheless, certain deliberate lies serve as a means of encoding unconscious truths; as such, a manifest lie may coexist with an unconscious truth.

The conscious liar tends to be exploitative and *parasitic* of others. He or she gratifies entirely selfish needs, usually at the expense of the recipient of his or her messages. This parasitic mode of relatedness is basic to the interactions of those who consciously deceive.

Despite these parasitic qualities (and in part because of them), many individuals are quite attracted to liars and their messages. Through unconscious identification, they share in the liar's pathological omnipotence and seeming ability to manipulate and control reality. They welcome the falsification of painful realities and the false belief that nothing can defeat the lying individual. On another level, such receivers fall willing victims to the hostility and destructiveness of the liar because of their own guilt-ridden (masochistic) needs for suffering. Still, it is mainly the false air of omnipotence that helps to reinforce the enormous seductive qualities of the deliberate liar.

The basic criterion of a lie or liar that will be used in this chapter is the means by which an individual deals with an emotionally charged trigger. The liar is someone who avoids or obliterates the multiple meanings of a stimulus and fails to respond to it with meaningful encoded expressions. Instead, he or she reacts in a way that destroys both the meaning of the precipitant and the response. Such a person does so by entirely sealing off the underlying truths and/or creating a substitute fiction (lie) that has no essential relationship to the activated meanings of the stimulus. A lie often serves as an impenetrable barrier to underlying truths; it is then called a *lie-barrier formation*. It has an enormously defensive function.

PSEUDO-INSIGHTS

For our purposes, liars can be identified only through their response to an emotionally charged trigger. Such individuals wish *not* to represent or experience meaning and truth. They wish *not* to work over the conscious and unconscious implications of a disturbing situation. Their main goal is to deny the presence of inner or outer disturbance and to seal off all possible ramifications. This type of adaptation through obliteration can at times provide relief to lie senders or receivers. Such individuals (patients and therapists as well as others) create elaborate fictions which they claim contain understanding of reality but which, upon analysis, prove devoid of true meaning. These are false or *pseudo-insights,* attractive lies generated unwittingly in the name of truth.

FAILURE TO RECOGNIZE LIES

There appear to be three major reasons why psychoanalysts and others have failed to recognize the existence of liars and obliterators (truth obliterators) as defined here. First, there is their overriding interest in the active pursuit of knowledge and understanding, a need to discover and assign meaning, that has been so intense as to create blind spots to the absence of meaning. Of course, it has been known that some persons manifestly have little wish to understand themselves and others, but the deeper need to destroy unconscious implication has been missed. This oversight has been supported by the ease with which analysts and therapists can propose implied or hidden meaning for virtually every communication from their patients.

A second and related reason for overlooking the widespread existence of truth obliterators is based on an inherent fear of the lie, its devastating consequences, and the power it affords those who use it effectively. This attitude is part of a general ambivalence toward lies in general, and it extends to a fear of those individuals who can somehow find relief from suffering through obliteration rather than meaningful coping. Because of the natural tendencies in all of us, the attractiveness of the liar is both threatening and dangerous. Often, those who receive lie messages respond with an unconscious truth-obliterating attitude of their own, through which they deny the existence of the falsifications involved.

Finally, it is our small or large tendencies toward lying which we must deny and which prompt us to deny similar tendencies in others. For example, psychoanalysts have long engaged in the proliferation of elaborate unconscious lies and fictions of which they have had some measure of realization, conscious or unconscious (mostly the latter). Because of their need to accept and believe in their own lie-barrier systems, they have failed to recognize such qualities in their patients' associations.

The lie, as noted, is an obliterating defense that may ease an emotionally charged situation for a particular person. It makes use of the defense of denial (and perhaps repression as well), provides concrete and direct satisfaction, and creates the illusion of having disposed of a problem. It is therefore inherently appealing and something we often turn to quite automatically, entirely outside of awareness.

Lie-barrier systems also preclude mature modes of related-ness with others and tend to require such relationship qualities as shared defenses, the mutual reinforcement of lie-barrier systems (a form of pathological symbiosis or nurturing), or the exploitation of others in order to maintain the unconscious lie system (the parasitic mode of relatedness). Individuals who make extensive use of lie-barrier systems can relate well only to those who share such beliefs (however unconsciously). The truth is persecutory for the liar (as it often is even for the truth teller or receiver). However, for the liar, the truth threatens to destroy all sense of equilibrium, a sense falsely gained through lie-barrier systems and unsound modes of adaptation.

For emotional problems and conscious and unconscious communicative interactions, there is but one truth, although there are many lies. Lies are often highly creative. They may also be rigid because of the liar's urgent need to maintain and elaborate fictions to prevent underlying truths from breaking through. Thus the liar is often under considerable pressure to maintain and even elaborate his or her barrier systems in the face of relentless (however intermittent) emotionally charged triggers.

NONDERIVATIVE LIES

Let us return to the situation faced by Peggy and George (in Chapter 15). Suppose that after his visit to the hospital, George had gone home to his five-year-old daughter. George told his daughter that her mother was fine, that she simply had to be away for a few days. He went on to say that because the weather was hot and sunny, he would take his daughter to the park. Grandmother would be coming to stay with them and to take care of her. Both Mommy and Daddy, he said, love their daughter very much.

Manifestly, each of these statements is essentially true. However, their main function for the moment is to seal off an underlying trigger and a set of chaotic truths that would be highly painful for George to communicate and for his daughter to hear. In this instance, we have what is called a *nonderivative lie-barrier* defense in that the surface of the message does not yield to meaningful decoding in light of the implications of the prevailing trigger. Thus the surface messages are *not derived* from the latent implications of the disturbing stimulus. The message contains manifest but not latent meaning.

Of course, if George's daughter then overheard a conversation about her mother's miscarriage, she would be quite unprepared and would probably have considerable difficulty in working over its ramifications. She would have the added burden of trying to understand why no one had told her about the incident or explained it to her. In addition, it is likely that even in the absence of any direct mention of the miscarriage, this particular trigger would influence the manifest exchanges between George and Peggy when she returned home. Their daughter would therefore be faced with a series of encoded messages that might have some discernible meaning manifestly, but that are more likely to evoke unconscious encoded responses that would be very troublesome for the child to deal with.

We see, then, that lies are immediately protective but unable to provide lasting adaptive resources and coping abilities. If George's daughter were inclined toward lie-barrier formations, she would reinforce her own defenses with those of her father. If, on the other hand, her inclination were to seek out and work over the truth, there would be a conflict of communicative needs.

DERIVATIVE LIES

Suppose, instead, that George told his daughter that everything was fine and that her mother would just be away for a few days getting some rest. George then suggested that because the weather was warm they should go to the beach and swim in the ocean. George then talked about the danger of drowning when the ocean gets rough and how sometimes even the strongest swimmers may succumb. He cautioned his daughter not to go out too far into the water and told her a sad story of how a child he once knew had drowned.

In this instance, there is still no manifest allusion to the miscarriage. On the other hand, in light of the trigger, the latter part of George's communications to his daughter contains an encoded working over of the miscarriage theme. This particular message could be viewed as an *encoded truth* or a *derivative lie-barrier formation*. In such a formation, the implication is that while the truth has been avoided directly, the surface message does indeed contain in disguised form representations of the underlying actualities. Thus in George's first set of messages he used the kind of defense that totally sealed off the underlying chaos; in his second he used more compromised expressions that included some reflection of underlying meaning.

There are, then, gradations of lie-barrier systems and of lies themselves. At the one extreme, there are those unconscious lies that exclude virtually all representations of a trigger; at the other extreme, there are those that contain ample encoded representations of the truth in the absence of any direct allusion to the stimulus and its meanings.

Individuals who make use of denial lie-barrier systems will either obliterate all reference to a trigger to exclude any thinly disguised representation of the stimulus. They may mention a trigger but will then produce a series of subsequent communications that do not contain meaningful encoded responses to that trigger.

LIE NARRATION

One final illustration: Suppose George, while driving home from the hospital, has a daydream in which he is walking in the street. He finds a $100 bill but gives it to a policeman. He meets his business partner, and they discuss a contract for some $50,000 worth of lumber. George mulls over the negotiations on the price and feels pleased that he would be able to get that much money for the deal. He thinks a great deal about the man who has purchased the lumber. He is easy to do business with, George thinks, although he sometimes negotiates a hard bargain.

In this daydream, there is no clearly discernible representation of the trigger, Peggy's miscarriage. The images do not organize around this particular stimulus, and they do not have evident encoded meaning in light of its implications. Extended fantasies of this kind, which have no bearing on activated triggers, have been called *lie-barrier narrations* and those who weave such tales, *lie narrators*. This particular daydream is clearly a nonderivative lie-barrier formation, one that effectively seals off the underlying chaos related to the miscarriage. Were this George's only response to the incident, he would have opted for massive obliterating defenses with little effort at active coping and working over. He would then be quite vulnerable to the intrusion of issues and representations related to the miscarriage and would have failed to resolve his inevitable sense of disturbance either consciously or unconsciously.

THE LIE SENDER

Since certain realistic and emotional truths are so enormously painful and even persecutory, it is not at all surprising that most individuals are prepared to obliterate a small or large portion of such truths. They do so in countless ways, many of them depending on the nature of the disturbing trigger and their own communicative and defensive propensities. There are many forms of conscious and unconscious pretense and an endless variety of lie systems and lie barriers that serve to obliterate, distract, falsify, magically deny, idealize in the face of disillusionment, and otherwise protect us from truths within ourselves, others, and life's disturbing moments. They are truths that we do not wish to cope with, consciously or unconsciously, in more direct fashion.

LIE SYSTEMS IN A CULTURE

Lie systems are often shared between individuals and within a particular culture. When two individuals make use of similar lie-barrier mechanisms, they tend to get along together quite well. If, on the other hand, there is a discordance between lie-barrier formations, there is likely to be considerable conflict.

In addition, there is always great stress between a truth obliterator and a truth teller. The former seems hollow and defensive to the latter; the latter is an enormous threat to the former. Liars require extensions of their lies; for them, the truth is persecutory and intolerable. Their basic mode of functioning depends upon the perpetuation of fictions and the avoidance of direct and encoded representations of triggers and meaningful reactions to them.

Politics, religion, various types of organizations, and even much that is taught in schools and universities frequently involve derivative and nonderivative (encoded and obliterating) unconscious lies. When someone dies, a child is told that he or she has gone to heaven and has found peace. When faced with a serious illness, we often engage in magical rituals and create magical beliefs that are supposed to guarantee our survival. Sometimes even in the face of a major catastrophe, our reaction is flat; we acknowledge the trigger but do little to work it over, not even daring to have a meaningful responsive dream.

In all of these situations, the issue is not one of surface truth or falsity. Instead, the focus is on responses to disturbing triggers that lead us to express messages essentially designed as barriers against underlying perceptions, fantasies, and the related affects and anxieties. Especially when realistic hope is out of the question, lie systems serve as a desperate recourse and often function quite mercifully and quite well. It is here that the adaptive value of lie systems can be recognized, though their misapplication to situations that would permit a more constructive resolution were they worked through (as seen with the usual emotionally disturbing trigger) can lead to highly fragile states of equilibrium that are quite vulnerable to breakdown. Often, immediate relief is gained at considerable cost, and the use of the lie system and denial spreads to many other areas to a point where overall functioning may be disturbed.

SHARING LIES

Suppose that George had walked into Peggy's hospital room and had greeted her as if nothing at all had happened. Suppose he had behaved as if he were coming home from a day's work and made no allusion whatsoever, directly or indirectly, to her miscarriage or even to the fact that she was in the hospital. He regales Peggy with the details of his day at work and with a variety of contractual issues. When Peggy happens to mention her obstetrician, George engages in extensive idealization, speaking of his large practice, his great bedside manner, his superb reputation, his charm as a person, and such.

In various ways, these would be lie-barrier messages with little derivative (encoded) function. In particular, the idealization of the obstetrician would constitute a specific lie-barrier system that Peggy might or might not share with her husband. If her own inclination were toward a working over of the truth of the situation, directly and through encoded messages, she would find George's comments intolerable. If her own lie-barrier preferences did not move in the direction of idealization, she would be irritated by her husband's statements. On the other hand, if she, too, made use of such overvaluation as a means of obliterating the truth, she would join in and extend the accolades.

COMMON TYPES OF UNCONSCIOUS LIARS ─────────

THE MINDLESS PERSON

There are several common types of lie communicators. The first can be termed the *mindless person.* In response to a disturbing trigger, his or her comments are boring and empty, essentially devoid of meaning on any level. Shallowness and flatness are striking, and his or her communicative expressions are superficial and without substance, manifest or latent. There is a sense of void. Blind action is common.

To illustrate, if George had spoken to Peggy in endless detail of a trivial incident at work or of an absurdly simple experience with his daughter, he would be functionally mindless and without meaningful response to the miscarriage trigger. In this type of lie-barrier noncommunication, there is a destruction of all meaningful relatedness with others.

The same effect is seen with unreasoned actions. If George had impulsively got drunk or rushed off to a house of prostitution, his behavior would reflect mindless actions and thoughtless efforts to destroy meaning and understanding.

With the mindless person, there is often a sense that his or her barriers are fragile and maintained at the cost of all sense of thought, creativity, warmth, and responsiveness. Such a person is experienced as a fragile nonentity and may at times actually seem provocative in his or her hollowness. This is especially true to the receivers of his or her message, who often feel, if they are involved in the trigger, that they are being treated as inconsequential and unimportant. Thus the mindless person destroys all expression of inner and outer meaning and seems absent though present.

THE CLICHÉ MAKER

The second common type of lie sender is the *cliché maker.* Clichés are an extremely common lie-barrier formation, many of them conveyed quite unconsciously. Those who are clever with the cliché make them seem to be substantial expressions, although closer examination reveals an essential absence of dynamic and vital meaning. For example, George might say to Peggy: "All is well that ends well; at least you have your health, and you can still have more children. Besides, it's good for the soul to sometimes go through an experience like this. It's part of being human. It could have been worse. You already have a child. Live and let live. Appreciate those you have, and let the past be the past. You are a strong woman; you can handle it. Wait and see, you'll bounce back and have twins."

The cliché maker can go on and on in this fashion. While there are no surface lies, clichés tend to address in some remote way the manifest aspects of a trigger. The clichés are worn thin with time and repetition and no longer have meaning. Even though George mentions the miscarriage, there is no impact, no sense of derivative or encoded communication, and no sense of meaningful coping. Still there is a reassuring quality to these words, which, though hollow, are often embraced by the message receiver. The pretense at meaning is welcomed as a lie-barrier formation that sets to the side a more compelling impact from underlying disturbing truths.

THE LIE NARRATOR

A third type of lie communicator, described above, is the *lie narrator* (or the *lie fictionalist*). This type of individual can be quite creative. His or her lie propensities will often go entirely unnoticed unless the receiver engages in an exercise in which the trigger for these messages is identified and analyzed and the messages themselves studied for representations of the stimulus and for encoded responses. It seems likely that a great deal of literature, daydreams, and personal tales are created in just this very way. In essence, the lie narrator weaves magnificent stories that are functionally designed as barriers to underlying painful truths and as lie systems that serve as a substitute for these more painful realizations.

To illustrate, suppose that George had entered Peggy's hospital room and said that on the way to the hospital he had mentally composed a short story which he had to tell her about. In brilliant and glowing detail he then recounted the story of a beautiful woman with a strange fixation: she was attracted only to men with a mole on their buttocks. With vivid images George described how, as a teenager, "This woman, in the course of petting with a male classmate, discovered such a mole and immediately surrendered her virginity to him with great orgastic pleasure. Her search for the mole soon became an obsession. If a boyfriend disrobed and revealed clear-skinned buttocks, she was turned off and rejected his further advances. But if he were the rare individual with a mole on his buttocks, she responded with overwhelming passion.

"In college, word of her obsession soon spread among the fraternities. Mole-buttocked men seemed to come out of the woodwork to pursue her, and clever upperclassmen found ingenious ways to produce artificial moles on their rear ends. Still, entreaties from her girlfriends could do little to stem her fixation.

"It all came to an unexpected and crushing end during a summer vacation. While spending a week with her parents at a seaside resort, one night she inadvertently opened the bathroom door. Suddenly she was confronted by her mother's buttocks: a dramatic mole stood on one cheek. In shock and terror, the poor girl, who had never entertained a conscious homosexual thought in her life, immediately lost her attraction for mole-buttocked men. Not to be dissuaded from her amorous adventures, she quickly became enthralled with left-handed men instead. An epidemic of ambidexterity soon broke out on her college campus. To this day, the dear girl has not realized that her mother is also left-handed."

Although it was perhaps a bit bizarre, George told this story with a flourish that was captivating to his audience. Even the nurse who had heard the beginning of his tale stayed on to the end, laughing and enjoying its absurdity. On the surface, the story seems to have an emotionally meaningful message: this is a tale in which we learn that sometimes unconscious homosexual wishes and fantasies can be a major determinant in the choice of heterosexual partners. Thus, the story has evident psychological meaning and wisdom. Because of this, certain lie narrations have been extremely difficult to recognize as such. Their surface implications have blinded us to the absence of encoded relevance to a currently disturbing trigger.

Although the tale is indeed sexual and has something to do with the relationship between a daughter and her mother, it has little evident encoded relevance to Peggy's miscarriage and its implications. There is little in the way of a representation of this trigger, of disguised perceptions and fantasies, or of other responses to the medical situation. The story itself, then, serves more as a means of obliterating the incident than of representing and working it over.

Because of the richness of their tales and their offer of functional lie-barrier formations, lie narrators are often admired and even idolized. They are clearly the most engaging type of lie communicator and make it quite possible for their listeners to deceive themselves into believing that important truths are being worked over. As noted, it is only by studying the relationship between the narration and the most critical emotional triggers that the true function of these tales can be determined.

THE LIE RECEIVER (TRUTH OBLITERATOR)

Lie receivers will not allow the truth contained in disturbing triggers to register meaningfully in their minds. They accomplish this feat by establishing sensory barriers to threatening incoming emotional stimuli. Or, once received, these inputs can be isolated, squeezed dry of meaning. They can deny their perceptions and/or their implications. Some of these people want to know nothing about nothing. If meaning registers or is acknowledged, on an encoded or direct level, it is almost immediately fragmented and destroyed. There is no lasting sense of true understanding in light of emotionally charged inputs.

Lie reception is reflected in the messages that a receiver imparts to the original sender. Thus most lie senders are also lie receivers.

When George ruminated about his work to his wife, Peggy, in the hospital room, he was functioning as a lie receiver and lie sender. Consciously and unconsciously his pretense was that the miscarriage had not happened. Sometimes such an effort can be quite intense; at other moments it can be maintained only as long as there is no reinforcement of the disturbing trigger. Thus, for example, if Peggy herself had brought up the miscarriage, George's maintenance of the defense would have depended on the extent to which he could work over its implications directly and indirectly or, instead, would have had to change the subject on all levels. If George acknowledged his concern about the miscarriage, mentioned his fantasy of rescuing the damsel in distress, but then would hear no more of the subject and shifted to mindless chatter, we would have an instance where he functioned momentarily as a truth receiver, only to change almost immediately into a truth obliterator.

The "pollyanna" and the cliché maker are often lie receivers, individuals who empty disturbing triggers of their traumatic qualities. The "pollyanna" replaces such hurts with good and positive images that are functionally false. Many seemingly naive individuals are also lie receivers, as are those who appear to be insensitive and self-centered.

In general, both the lie receiver and the lie sender sacrifice an important measure (and sometimes the totality) of meaningful relatedness. They show communicative failures in both sending and receiving messages. They are difficult to reach, typically unhelpful to others, and impossible to engage in serious communicative exchanges. Dynamically, lie-barrier tendencies are based on many factors, such as envy, hostility, defenses against sexual fantasies, narcissistic (self-image) disturbances, genetic (childhood) contributions, and more.

Although individuals tend to have a fundamental style of sending and receiving messages, under especially trying conditions a truth communicator may resort to lies and barriers. This change tends to be rather rare, although the reverse, a lie communicator shifting to the truth, appears more common (especially in response to heavily charged emotional triggers). In particular, when there is a major disturbance in a person's basic security or holding relationship, and when the fundamental conditions and rules of relatedness with a particular individual are altered, most individuals will work over the triggers involved with truthful encoded expressions. This type of response occurs because of our basic needs for consistent caring and containment and for clear rules of interaction and relatedness. Since these needs are fundamental to our sense of security and identity and to our relationships with others, disturbances in these areas are likely to evoke active, truthful, coping responses.

Lie systems tend to be intriguing and appealing. They are extremely common because of the harsh realities of life. Lies have their assets and their liabilities. An individual requires a special capability to overcome his or her natural tendencies in this direction.

CHAPTER 17
DUMPERS

As we have seen, the basic distinction between communicators is whether they deal meaningfully with underlying emotional problems or obliterate them. In discussing liars and truth tellers, we have been dealing with what can be termed *quiet messages*. These are communicative expressions in which the main power of the message lies in its meaning or absence of meaning, with little in the way of interpersonal pressure and charge. Although feelings may be involved, the message itself can be subjected to quiet contemplation without a sense of tension.

There is, however, another style of communicating that is immediately pressured and itself emotionally charged. The receiver of such messages feels disturbed or aroused, dumped into, agitated, and stirred up. These are *noisy messages*, difficult to contemplate and contain, and likely to evoke intense reactions.

Individuals who generate messages of this kind are called *dumpers*. (Technically, they are said to use *projective identification*.) Quite unconsciously, they make use of messages in order to get rid of something disturbing within themselves by placing it into, pushing it into, or dumping it into a receiver. This goal stands in contrast to the wish to impart meaning, to be understood, or to obliterate meaningful response. The main goal, then, is that of discharge and the riddance of disturbing inner tensions, fantasies, perceptions, and the like. The goal is therefore to create a comparable disturbance in another person (through which the sender imagines that the problem can be eliminated). At times the hope is to create a sense of turbulence in the other individual so he or she will then work over the disturbing evacuated and incorporated contents in a more effective fashion than possible for the sender. Under the latter circumstances, the receiver or *container* for a dump-message (the *contained*) will generate responsive messages that reflect his or her better coping capacities. These reactive communications are then experienced by the original dumper in a manner that permits the incorporation of the other person's better functioning. As a result, the original dumper is better able to manage his or her disturbing inner state. Thus, dumping may be geared toward hurting and disturbing another person or toward gaining his or her assistance with unmanageable inner problems.

For dumpers, language and affect are used not for understanding or defense but for discharge and evacuation. Dumpers' unique form of expression has been recognized slowly because of the initial assumption that the use of words implies an expression of meaning and a pursuit of understanding. While it has been known that some actions are designed for the discharge of anxiety, conflict, and the like, the use of words for this purpose has gained recognition only in recent years.

TRUTH DUMPERS AND LIE DUMPERS

There are two kinds of dumpers: truth dumpers and lie dumpers. Thus there are dumpers whose accompanying communications do indeed represent meaningful triggers and encoded responses to them. Such individuals, *truth dumpers*, wish both to get rid of inner disturbance and to understand the nature of their inner and interpersonal struggles. While dumping is their primary purpose, meaningful communication and understanding are also possible.

In contrast, the *lie dumper* wishes only to evacuate highly charged inner contents and is not in the least interested in understanding the relevant meaning and implications. Lie dumpers wish only to evacuate what disturbs them and to stir up those who receive their messages. As a rule, such dumping is extremely violent, agitating, and highly destructive. The relationship between the dumper and the container (receiver) is highly parasitic in that the lie dumper wishes only to exploit others with little regard for their needs. Efforts by those who are the targets for such messages to try to understand the nature of the situation are met by the dumper with a near-total lack of receptivity. The fully absorbed lie dumper has no interest in understanding his or her own messages or those of others and is in a virtually unassailable communicative space. In general, the listener must first work over and modify the dumping propensity itself before making any attempt to understand the underlying issues involved.

METABOLISM

Dumping requires containing and working over of incorporated contents and intentions, issues that do not arise with quiet communication. This working over process is called *metabolism* and should be geared toward understanding the unconscious implications of the extruded contents. It is therefore quite important to recognize those situations in which action and language are being used for this purpose and to respond accordingly. In this regard, it is essential to rely on one's sensitivity to being stirred up and dumped into. It is also essential to develop safeguards against reading these qualities improperly into a communicative interchange. Some individuals constantly feel put upon and dumped, no matter the sender's intention.

Lie dumpers are often violently provocative and unreachable. They tend to be highly narcissistic and selfish individuals, quite agitated, and attempt to cope by creating agitation in others. They have little sympathy for their receivers and little concern for the emotions and turmoil they create within them. They are capable of arousing intense feelings of rage, sexuality, and guilt but can seem relatively detached themselves. At other times, their own agitation is quite evident. Their preferred method of coping is to agitate their receivers in the unconscious hope of magically ridding themselves, however momentarily, of their own inner tensions.

DUMP RECEIVERS ARE DUMP SENDERS ⎯⎯⎯⎯⎯⎯⎯⎯

Dump senders tend to be dump receivers. They take in quiet messages and almost immediately attempt violently to rid themselves of their implications. They respond to truthful communication with a violent destruction of the meaning and with agitated communications of their own. Little effort is made to process received messages toward understanding or modulated response. There is virtually no tolerance of inner tension, and since the truth tends to build anxiety, a dumper's responses tend to be quite immediate and quite violent.

The dump receiver is, of course, a poor listener and some-one with very little capacity for sympathy or empathy. Dump receivers are difficult to be with, a constant source of disturbance, and persons with whom it is difficult to contain one's own inevitable reactions toward dump responses.

In general, the dump sender and the dump receiver are attempting to maintain a fragile equilibrium through riddance measures. They are usually quite ill emotionally, people who have had little in the way of steady holding, containing, and maternal care. Their mother figure tends to have lacked the capacity for *reverie*, an ability to take in early and primitive dumping messages from an infant, to work them over through metabolism, and to return them to the child in a soothing way. The child as a result has difficulty in the internal holding and containing necessary to produce quiet messages. Still it is well to remember that dumping is an effort at self-cure through immediate tension relief, however crude. It is a special mode of adaptation that must itself be modified if more quiet forms of understanding are to develop.

On the whole, dumping is a maladaptive communicative style. It tends to preclude or interfere with mature relatedness; it is so focused on action and discharge that growth and emotional maturation are virtually impossible. Dumping creates communicative and interpersonal alienation and antagonism. It often involves psychologically violent attacks on the receiver and sometimes spills over into actual physical assaults. As a result, there can be no sense of trust, mutuality, respect and concern in a relationship with a dumper. Because dumping is inimical to any type of adaptive solution to internal and interpersonal conflicts and anxieties, it cannot bring lasting peace to those who use it. It is nonetheless a communicative style to which such persons repeatedly turn in the face of stressful triggers, sometimes doing so against their conscious wishes.

Dumpers never seem to grow and learn, to bind tensions, to reflect. They are prisoners in their own communicative chains; only rarely do such people experience true communicative freedom. They often yearn deeply for receivers who will contain what they must extrude, though they seldom show gratitude for such responses.

Some emotionally charged situations are inherently filled with dumping qualities. A sudden miscarriage, for example, is bound to stir up those involved. To illustrate, let us once more turn to George and Peggy. Agitated by the miscarriage, suppose George had come into his wife's hospital room criticizing and verbally attacking the obstetrician. Peggy's belief in the doctor is shaken, and she picks up her husband's blind rage. When Peggy tries to reassure George, he attacks her directly and accuses her of always being against him and trying to defend those who are indefensible. Peggy begins to feel guilty over what she has done and becomes depressed.

Here, George has dumped into his wife his own sense of violence, guilt, and depression, unconsciously hoping to be rid of his own inner disturbance and to place it into his wife. If Peggy had become overtly guilt-ridden and depressed, George might have begun to feel better. He might have initiated efforts to help his wife with her disturbance. In this way, he would have gained both distance and distraction from his own inner difficulty, and he would have created a way to manage his own inner disturbance, now placed into his wife.

Whether George would be a truth dumper or lie dumper would depend on the nature of his accompanying communications. If they did indeed contain encoded messages related to the miscarriage, the former would apply; in contrast, if there were no meaningful disguised expressions, the latter would be the case.

In general, if Peggy were to react directly to George's dumping with efforts to placate him or to help him understand the situation, George would probably become more agitated and would intensify his dumping efforts. Instead, it would be crucial for Peggy first to address George's efforts at action and evacuation and to call these to his attention. She might be able to point out how little is to be gained in this way and even suggest a quieter form of struggling communication. In any case, the dumping issue must be considered before any matters of content. Failure to do so will usually insure the continuation of the dumping communicative style in the sender.

Overall, then, dumping is maladaptive and pathological and requires a special form of message reception and response. It is extremely important to recognize such tendencies within ourselves and to attempt to contain and manage them on our own. Recognizing dumping in others can foster effective communicative reactions. A failure to recognize this particular mode of communication often leads to total communicative misunderstanding and personal alienation.

CHAPTER 18

ROLE AND IMAGE EVOCATIONS

There remains one final dimension of communication for us to study. It, too, involves efforts by a message sender to arouse a response in a message receiver. However, the issue here is not one of dumping and riddance, but instead an attempt to *evoke* a particular kind of behavior, role, or self-image in the other person. It is a dimension of human communication that does not involve the issue of meaning or its absence, but which instead is highly interpersonal and interactional.

Unconsciously, a sender's message may be designed to generate in a receiver an enormous range of feelings, fantasies, perceptions, and behaviors. These may extend into efforts to have the receiver experience himself or herself in a particular way or to adopt a special attitude or role. While some of these efforts may be quite deliberate, their most important expressions are outside of the awareness of the sender—and often the receiver as well.

Since the experience of a role and image evocation in another person's message is an entirely subjective evaluation on the part of the receiver, these impressions must once again be approached with considerable caution. It is all too easy whenever we feel a particular way or do something in interacting with another person to blame him or her for creating the state within ourselves. Under all circumstances, role and image evocations are an interactional product of the messages imparted and the propensities of the message receiver. Sometimes the message itself is the major determinant of the resultant image and behavior; sometimes the tendencies of the receiver have the overriding influence in response to a relatively innocuous trigger. All such feelings and impressions must be analyzed and reanalyzed and special efforts made to sort out the contributions from both sides of a communicative exchange.

For example, on a manifest level, we may try to blame people to make them feel guilty, to render them helpless, or to arouse them sexually or aggressively. We may extend these efforts and try to have them enact a sexual or aggressive fantasy or have them behave in a particularly contrite, angry, seductive, or other way. Even when these provocations are conscious, we must always analyze their unconscious sources within ourselves. Usually a sender generates an encoded message with pressures of this kind of which both he or she and the receiver are unaware. The receiver suddenly experiences a sense of guilt or acts in hostile fashion, not realizing the extent to which the response has been provoked by received, encoded messages. It is on this level that many disturbing interpersonal transactions take place.

However, not all role and image evocations have a negative cast. Consciously, and often quite unconsciously, we also endeavor to mobilize in others constructive responses, adaptive behaviors, and positive images. Pressures of this kind are inevitable in most meaningful communicative exchanges.

In general, emotionally charged triggers evoke the encoded messages that contain role and image evocations. Thus to fully comprehend this dimension of human communication we must once more identify its triggers.

There are many familiar patterns of role and image evocation. When a particular trigger makes us feel helpless, we respond with direct and encoded communications. We try either to make others feel similarly inept or to have them adopt a strong role through which we obtain support. Often when we ourselves feel guilty over a particular act or fantasy, we will attempt unconsciously to goad others into actions that could evoke within them guilt or a feeling of undue badness.

AN ILLUSTRATION WITH ASPECTS OF DUMPING ──────

To cite an example, we will return one last time to George and his wife. At work, in dealing with a man who was negotiating for the purchase of lumber, George became irritated and provocative. He was inconsistent in his proposals and his client was soon quite confused. The client's responsive messages reflected his state of uncertainty. In this instance, George has managed to arouse in his client, the receiver, a state of uncertainty and disturbance not unlike his own inner turmoil. There is some measure of dumping as well as role and image evocations. The client quickly developed an image of himself as quite helpless, much of it unconsciously evoked through George's messages to him.

In further negotiations, George kept questioning his client's veracity in demanding certain concessions. The client soon felt guilty for the position that he had taken in the negotiations, a self-image that had been promoted by George's encoded expressions. When George grew directly provocative, the client felt himself to be the victim. In this way, George both dumped his own sense of victimization into his client and evoked self-images of a type with which he himself was struggling. It can be readily seen that a full comprehension of interpersonal pressures of this kind can develop only through an understanding of their immediate triggers.

Role and image evocations are communicative expressions with strong dynamic and genetic implications. They often are the consequence of attempts to cope with internal conflict and anxiety and touch upon issues for both sender and receiver that have strong echoes into the past. Still, the recognition of such pressures, understood in light of a careful evaluation of their sources, leads to comprehension of an important dimension of our communicative lives.

CHAPTER 19

COMMUNICATIVE STYLES IN DAILY INTERACTIONS

An important aspect of self-knowledge involves the identification of one's own preferred mode of communication. In this determination, it is essential to analyze the ways in which we react to emotionally charged triggers in terms of their conscious and unconscious implications. In evaluating the communicative styles of others, the same technique should be applied, though it must be carried out as part of a truthful mode of expression lest the impressions involved prove to be erroneous.

THE IMPORTANCE OF QUIET REFLECTION

It is of considerable value to pause after an emotionally meaningful interlude to identify and analyze the triggers and to explore our responses to them. In this way, it is possible not only to determine one's own communicative propensities, but also to identify the specific encoded messages with which we have responded to such stimuli. Such an effort often provides us with unexpected insights into our view of and reaction to emotionally meaningful situations. These endeavors can be supplemented by taking time when alone, such as just before falling asleep, to permit ourselves a period of free association and exploration. At some point, such meanderings are brought into focus and analyzed through an identification of the important traumatic triggers of the day, and the associations at hand are studied in terms of encoded responses to these precipitants. In general, it is always best to consider encoded *perceptions* of the actual attributes of others and their triggers before thinking about reactive fantasies and other adaptive responses.

Efforts of this kind often help us to understand an odd experience or an emotional symptom, an otherwise inexplicable piece of behavior, or some other reaction that appears to be emotionally founded. Since the sources of inappropriate responses lie within our unconscious fantasies and perceptions, trigger decoding helps us to gain access to the unconscious basis for such disturbances. Again, as long as we maintain an internal attitude of truth sending and truth receiving, the insights gained in this way can be considerable.

In these efforts it is always helpful to permit our associations to wander back to earlier childhood experiences that could help account for particular sensitivities and to specific reactions to emotionally charged triggers. No period of self-analysis of this kind, of communicative understanding, is complete until all of the emotionally charged triggers have been identified and analyzed, the major encoded responses recognized, and the connection to childhood events and relationships brought into perspective.

In the course of such efforts, it is necessary to consistently struggle against the inevitable human tendency for defense and obliteration. Awareness of possible resistances prepares us to struggle with them and leads us to search for triggers we try to avoid, perceptions we prefer not to register, and fantasies which we might just as well exclude. The freer the initial associating process in such efforts and the more careful, specific, and comprehensive the ultimate analysis, the likelier the resultant conscious decoding will prove meaningful and adaptive. It is important, then, to permit an extended period of free association before turning to efforts at analysis. Alternation between the two attitudes is also particularly helpful.

ACHIEVING INSIGHT THROUGH REFLECTION

For example, John is a manufacturer of men's suits. He discovers that Len, his purchasing officer, has been taking kickbacks from his suppliers. There is a terrible confrontation, during which Len reminds John of some of his own dishonest doings. Helplessly afraid of being found out himself, John does not fire Len, but warns him that any future dishonesty will lead to the termination of his employment.

Through the rest of the day and into the night, and while lying in bed before going to sleep, John goes over this experience again and again, quite consciously. That evening, when he discovers that his ten-year-old son has taken five dollars from his wallet, John attacks him mercilessly and subjects him to an extreme physical beating. Afterwards, he regrets his own loss of control and the extreme quality of his reaction.

As John lies in bed reviewing the day's events, he is well aware that the incident with Len was an emotionally traumatic trigger. He knows too that he felt helpless to deal with the situation because of his own dishonesty in business. He recognizes that he was angry with Len and regrets having done things that compromised his position.

John's experience with his son leads to some additional associations before he falls asleep. John thinks of how furious he is at himself for his own dishonesty. He has a daydream of restructuring his business honestly and of giving up the web of secret deals and false statements that have entrapped him.

After elaborating upon these themes, John suddenly realizes that they are a direct and encoded response to the experience with Len and a factor in his attack on his son. It becomes clear that he has tried to dump some of his own guilt into his child and that even though his son willingly lent himself to this need (as is so often the case), his reactions had been overstated. The attack on his son was also an encoded message that contained John's own rage toward himself and was meant to convey to his son that he should behave honestly and replace his dishonest self-image with one containing more integrity. Yet at the very time John was trying to teach his son self-control and restraint, he communicated a contradictory encoded message through his own behavior, one that stressed loss of control and impulsivity.

John lets his mind wander again. Suddenly he has an image of his father, who is now retired and living in California. He recalls his last visit to his parents' home. It had been hollow but not unpleasant. Next, he thinks of Larry, a close friend who is having an illicit affair. John suddenly remembers an incident in his childhood when he had overheard an hysterical battle between his parents. He suspected from the fragments that reached his ears that his mother was accusing his father of having had an affair. He hadn't recalled that particular memory in some years; in itself it has quite an unreal quality. He remembers having felt helpless then, as now, and realizes that he had been unable to bring up the subject with his parents and had never determined what had really happened.

John now pauses to take a look at his associations in light of the two triggers: the incidents with Len and his son. He now realizes that these events not only brought up his own burdensome dishonesty, but quite unconsciously had touched upon his doubts about his father. Contained here were some of the actual roots of John's own dishonest tendencies as well as part of the basis for his fury at his son. John now recognizes that his rage at his youngster had been a condensed expression of his anger at Len, himself, his father, and his son.

John now realizes another trigger for his behavior toward his son and for his sense of anxiety that day. He had hired a new secretary who was quite attractive and who had been blatantly seductive earlier that day. He had felt quite stimulated but also conflicted about whether to get involved with her. In the past, occasional affairs had made him feel very guilty and uncomfortable, and he had quickly broken them off. He thought that an experience of that kind with his new secretary might unduly complicate his life.

So here was another repressed trigger: his secretary's seductiveness. It had generated lascivious fantasies and guilt in John, and these had evoked additional guilt, anxiety, and conflict. To the extent that he was interested in his secretary, John was both stimulated and angry with himself. His perceptions of the secertary and of his responsive fantasies and wishes had led him to feel corrupt. This feeling had influenced his reactions to Len and his son. Again the genetic connection involved the childhood memory about his father. In all, this sequence of realized insights enabled John to cope far better with all concerned in the days that followed.

PROCEDURES FOR SELF-ANALYSIS ─────────────

The success of efforts of this kind depend upon the deliberate use of conscious decoding, the key to truth receiving. However, it is impossible to consciously control one's own communicated messages. Because of this, they may well contain meaningful encoded responses to triggers that prove to be analyzable, or they may fail to do so. If a period of self-analysis fails to yield significant encoded revelations of considerable surprise, it is safe to assume that one is making use of the lie-barrier communicative modality. It is often a sign of massive defensiveness. At times it proves possible to engage in further self-exploration in an effort to understand the underlying reasons for this defensive position. If this type of analysis proves successful, it is entirely possible unconsciously to then change the quality of one's associations so that they begin to reveal disguised representations of the emotional issues at hand. If the effort to modify one's defenses fails, it is best to allow a period of rest—of lying fallow—before trying another period of active self-analysis.

Often, the shift to the lie-barrier mode is prompted by dread of being overwhelmed by the truths in the triggers at hand. It is mainly when we fear intense regression, psychotic decompensation, or being overwhelmed—madness—that we invoke the most rigid lie-barrier systems we can muster. On the other hand, when we are disturbed and yet feel unconsciously that we can cope with the aroused issues, we tend to shift to truth sending and truth receiving.

DUMPING AS INIMICAL TO SELF-ANALYSIS ────────

In general, if we engage in intensive efforts at dumping during the day, our attempt at self-analysis will tend to fall flat. If we have evacuated and discharged the problem, we are quite disinclined, even unconsciously, to work over the underlying issues. Truth sending, truth receiving, and sound self-analysis require delay and tolerance of frustration of a kind inimical to dumping.

It requires a special effort for a lie sender or lie receiver to identify his or her own communicative style. By definition, this realization is impossible as long as the truth-obliterating style is in use. Still, a deliberate effort at identifying triggers and exploring associative responses can make such a determination feasible. One has to be on constant guard for the obliteration of important triggers and for a tendency to read meaning into essentially nonmeaningful (nonencoded) narrative expressions.

A momentary insight into lying tendencies can lead to some measure of conscious working over of this particular communicative style. It is possible to enforce delay, free association, and direct exploration of triggers, their implications, and our responses to them. It is therefore possible to some extent to modify one's own communicative defenses, to control tendencies toward dumping, and to provide an opportunity for more truthful sending and receiving. At times, these shifts can be carried over to relatively spontaneous exchanges with others.

THE INTERPLAY OF COMMUNICATIVE STYLES ─────────

In general, it is easier to identify the communicative style of someone else than our own. There is a more impartial sense of the analysis involved, though the principles are identical: the identification of a trigger and its implications, and deliberate efforts at conscious decoding designed to determine the presence of responsive disguised and meaningful messages.

The identification of someone else's communicative style relies, of course, on our own use of truth sending and truth receiving. The truth obliterator will either be disinclined to engage in an exercise of this kind or will do so in such a defensive fashion as to not arrive at a sound evaluation. The dumper will be so busy evacuating that he or she will have little or no interest in the issue at all.

Still one of the most critical determinants of our relationship with others is the communicative style of all concerned. It is essential in dealing with others to mobilize the truthful mode of communication and to then identify the specific communicative propensities of the other person. It is only the truth sender and receiver who can suitably adjust to the various kinds of possible interactions—those with other truth senders and receivers, those with liars, and those with dumpers. Truthful communicators are capable of considerably more flexibility than those who have the unconscious need to lie.

TWO TRUTH COMMUNICATORS

In general, the truthful sender and receiver will express himself or herself with sensitivity and tact with another truthful sender and receiver. There will be a sense of mutual understanding, and traumatic triggers will evoke meaningfully encoded reactions on both sides. Both individuals can engage in conscious decoding and react to each other in terms of both conscious and unconscious truths. There will be consistency within all levels of expression from both individuals and a basis for honesty and trust. While sometimes painful (and, as noted, tact must always be maintained), relationships of this kind show the smallest possible quota of psychopathology and provide the greatest measure of mature understanding and gratification. If an issue arises, it can be expected that most often the individuals involved will work it over consciously and unconsciously, and both will ultimately grow through understanding.

TRUTH COMMUNICATORS AND TRUTH OBLITERATOR

A truthful communicator will have some difficulty in relating to the liar. He or she will tend to be disturbed or put off by the latter's clichés, emptiness, distance, and meaningless narrations. He or she will sense the liar's needs for barriers and protection, interpersonal distance, and communicative aloofness. He or she will eventually recognize that there can be no meaningful exchange of feelings and ideas with such a person. If meaningful communication is desired, the truth teller must first attempt to help the lie communicator to become aware of his or her communicative style and its disadvantages. Some effort can be made to help the lie person modify his or her mode of expression, although since much of this style is unconsciously determined these efforts often have to be restricted to some measure of conscious decoding accompanied by an openness to its results.

The truth communicator will be wise not to attempt to press for meaningful expression in the presence of a lie communicator. While some effort in this direction may be carried out, the basic problem lies in the use of a fundamental mode of communication which negates the impact of the contents of the communicative exchanges. It is for this reason, among others, that the communicative style issue must be worked over first before effective communication can be established.

The truth communicator will, in general, be unable to reach the dumper, especially the lie dumper. He or she will recognize that dumping precludes meaningful interaction and that first it is necessary to contain the dumpings and show a capacity for tolerance. More meaningful efforts would have to be directed gently toward the recognition and modification of the dumping style of expression if a meaningful relationship and interchange are to develop. Helping the dumper develop controls, to manage his or her own tensions, and to become a bit reflective is essential. Often the dumper is an extremely troubled person in need of professional help. Short of such a measure, the truth receiver's ability to contain whatever is dumped into him or her and to metabolize it toward understanding and to then respond with an expression that is far less disturbing, will often prove quite helpful.

The lie communicator will have little tolerance for the truth sender and receiver. Such persons are for him or her quite threatening and persecutory as are their underlying expressed truths. The liar is therefore quite uncomfortable with the truth teller. Often the truth communicator intensifies the liar's need for falsifications and barriers.

TWO LIE COMMUNICATORS

When two lie communicators come together, the situation is uncertain. As noted, if their major lie systems correspond and support each other, they will tend to do very well together. They will share avoidance and defenses, and they will tend to ignore the falseness that characterizes their relationship. Each will maintain a tacit, unconscious agreement to avoid emotionally charged triggers and meaningful responses.

On the other hand, when their lie systems conflict, their relationship will contain a great deal of tension and hostility.

There may be a sudden interruption, frequent periods of misunderstanding, or pressures on each individual to shift his or her defensive style in keeping with that used by the other person. Still, many lie communicators develop fragile but lasting relationships with each other, virtually never examining the false foundations on which they are built.

DUMPERS AND OTHERS

The lie communicator is especially threatened by the dumper (truth or lie) whose efforts deeply challenge his or her own equilibrium and fragile defensive barriers. Liars therefore tend to be poor containers of dumping and tend to take flight from such relationships and from the stirrings that they evoke.

Finally, the lie dumper will often try to use the truth receiver as a safe container of his or her own inner disturbance. Much of his or her attitude is exploitative, but a relationship can be maintained nonetheless—especially if it is sadomasochistic (i.e., between someone who is sadistically exploitative and someone who is masochistically in need of exploitation). On the other hand, the truth dumper tends to get along well with the truth receiver, in part through shared understanding and in part by benefiting from the containing capacities of this kind of message recipient.

On the whole, a dumper is relatively intolerant of lie communicators, since dumpers are individuals who usually are refractory to containing whatever is placed into them because of its potentially disturbing qualities. Dumpers therefore do not get along well with liars, although occasionally they will take in a lie-barrier system from a liar and erect it around an agitated inner disturbance, thereby benefiting from the interaction.

Most utterly chaotic relationships are based on the bringing together of two dumpers, especially if they are lie dumpers. Each individual wishes to exploit the other and to blindly get rid of his or her disturbance by evacuating it into the other individual. There is usually a furious exchange of dumping with no meaningful containing. The sadomasochistic satisfactions can be quite enormous. Because of the unpredictable and fragile qualities involved, this type of exchange can also lead to the harm and withdrawal of one or both individuals.

In every meaningful personal relationship, it is critical to identify your own and the other person's communicative style. If meaning prevails, then meaning can be exchanged. If lies are involved, they can be recognized and modified. If dumping is the issue, then meaning must be set aside, however temporarily, and the response must first be contained. In general, all reactions to another person must be in keeping with his or her prevailing communicative style. Most problems in communication arise because of unrecognized but significant differences in the communicative styles of two persons. If truly meaningful exchanges are to take place, not only must two individuals share the same communicative space (style), but they must also eventually function as both truth senders and truth receivers.

THE COMMUNICATIVE STYLE OF THIS BOOK

An effort has been made in this volume to impart truth and meaning and to forgo as much as humanly possible any need to dump or to obliterate. It is very much hoped that the reader has accepted the messages manifest and encoded in this volume in open fashion, as a truth receiver. On that basis, it may well be that fresh insights into the nature of human communication, especially as it operates outside of awareness, have been generated. With self-analysis, the reader might find himself or herself in a better position to gain access to the truths involved and to benefit from their delineation.

There is evidence that we all possess inherently powerful tendencies to represent and seek the truth as it pertains to that which disturbs us, intrapsychically and interpersonally. This tendency finds powerful opposition in another inherent trend which forms the foundation for self-protection, defensiveness, and the immediate obliteration of pain and threat. This type of divided interest—of splitting—within the human mind is fateful indeed. Depending upon a wide range of factors (interpersonal, environmental, and personal), some of us become truth tellers, while others become liars. Nonetheless, for all individuals, it requires considerable determination and self-understanding and a remarkable capacity to tolerate pain and frustration, to maintain a relatively consistent investment in the unconscious truths of all emotional situations. Even the most natural truth teller may momentarily shift to a lie position when under duress.

In all, it is well for us to maintain a perspective on the human need for both lie and truth. It is far too easy (and almost a cliché or lie barrier) to state that in truth there is freedom and growth, while in lies there are only vulnerable protection and stultification. Far more meaningful is the realization that it is in the very nature of the human condition to struggle with truth and lie, conscious and unconscious. The lie communicator should have our sympathy and understanding; the truth teller, our deep admiration.

REFERENCES

Bion, W. (1977). *Seven Servants*. New York: Jason Aronson.

Freud, S. (1900). The interpretation of dreams. *Standard Edition* 4/5:1–627.

—— (1915). Repression. *Standard Edition* 14:141–158.

Khan, M. (1973). The role of illusion in the analytic space and process. *The Annual of Psychoanalysis* 1:231–246.

Langs, R. (1978). *The Listening Process*. New York: Jason Aronson.

—— (1979). *The Therapeutic Environment*. New York: Jason Aronson.

—— (1980). *Interactions: The Realm of Transference and Countertransference*. New York: Jason Aronson.

—— (1981). *Resistances and Interventions: The Nature of Therapeutic Work*. New York: Jason Aronson.

—— (1982a). *Psychotherapy: A Basic Text*. New York: Jason Aronson.

—— (1982b). *The Psychotherapeutic Conspiracy*. New York: Jason Aronson.

INDEX

Analytic hour, 134–143
Anxiety, 33
Associations, constellations of,
    136

Babel, Tower of, 10–11
Bion, W. R., 147

Child, as communicator, 12–14
Cliché maker, 170–171
Commensal relationship, 159
Commonsense meaning, 24
Communication
    encoded, 3–4
    etymology of, 18
    by infants, 12
    versus meaning, 49–50
    versus message, 18
    nonverbal, 22
    parables of, 10–12
    quiet, 151
    styles of, 8, 147–152, 196–197
        in daily interactions,

187–197
    and survival, 10
    transversal, 105
    unique, 106–107
Communicative alienation, 24
Communicative closeness, 24
Communicative unit, 9
Condensation, 34, 58, 59, 121,
    123
Consensual validation, 28–29
Contained, the, 178
Container, the, 178
Context, 21
    triggers and, 50–51
Contextual meaning, 24
Countertransference, 90

Day residue, 8, 61–62
Decoding, 89
    contextual, see Trigger
        decoding
    direct, 90–95
        of dreams, 111–117

Decoding (*continued*)
  inference, 92–94
  trigger, *see* Trigger decoding
  under and over, 79–80
Defense
  inevitable tendency for, 188
  nonderivative lie-barrier, 165
  and painful truths, 153
  paradoxical nature of, 3
Derivative(s), 44–47
  close, 45
  coalescible, 100
  coalescing, 105–106
  distant, 45
  less disguised, 104–105
Displacement, 34, 57, 60, 123
Dreams, 61–67
  of children, 14
  direct decoding of, 111–117
  dreamer and, 112–113
  Irma, 7–8
  responding to surface of,
    113–117
  trigger decoding of, 119–127
  unconscious expression in,
    36–37
Dream thoughts, 61
Dream work, 61
Drugs, and primary process, 35
Dumping, 151, 177–182
  inimical to self-analysis,
    191–192
  and lie communicators,
    195–196

Encoding
  conscious vertical, 43–44
  deliberate, 41–43, 51
  as emotional protection, 4
  horizontal, 43
  mechanisms working together,
    51–53
  preliminary conscious, 71

unconscious, *see* Unconscious
  encoding
Evocation, 183–185

Fantasy
  conscious versus unconscious,
    126–127
  raw inner, 50
  sexual, 153–154
  triggers for, 38
Fiction, 115
Fight or flight, 154
Freud, S., 32, 37, 44, 55
  The Interpretation of Dreams,
    7, 61–67, 80, 89, 111
  Irma, dream of, 7–8
  self-analysis of, 62–64
  and unconscious encoding,
    61–67
Freudian slips, 39, 85
Functional capacity (of a
  message), 55

Hypnotism, 39

Image evocation, 183–185
Inference decoding, 92–94
Inferences, 5, 92
Inherent meaning, 24
Insight
  dangers of, 11–12
  pseudo-, 163
  through reflection, 188–190
Internal dialogue, 23
Interpretation, 106–107
  encoded validation of,
    141–142
The Interpretation of Dreams
  (Freud), 7, 61–67, 80, 89,
  111

Joseph (Biblical), 11

Khan, M., 147

Latent contents, 20
Liar, parasitic, 162
Lie(s), 161
    and coping, 14
    in a culture, 168–169
    derivative, 166–167
    failure to recognize, 163–165
    nonderivative, 165–166
    sharing, 169
Lie-barrier, 163–164
    nonderivative, 165
Lie communicators, 170–173,
        194–195
    dumping and, 195–196
Lie dumpers, 178–179, 181–182
Lie narration, 167, 171–173
Lie receiver, 149, 161–175
Lie sender, 149, 161–175
Lying fallow, 191

Manifest content, 20
Meaning
    communication versus, 49–50
    destruction of, 147–148
    in messages, 24
    verifiable, 41
Mental world outside awareness,
        37–38
Message(s), 9
    versus communication, 18
    in context, 21
    contradictory, 83–84
    derivative, 44–47
    discord between intended and
        received, 84–85
    in discord with reality, 82–83
    with emotional contents, 86
    and emotional symptoms,
        86–87
    encoded, 27
        responding to, 47–49

etymology of, 17–18
forms of, 22
    special, 87–88
functional capacity of, 55
hidden, 130–132
    signs of, 81–88
ideal mixture of, 15
inner- and outer-directed,
    23–24
in isolation, 18–21
manifest, 27
meaning in, 24–25
motives behind, 23
quiet and noisy, 177–178
single and multiple, 13–14
true and false, 25–27
types of, 31–32
Metabolism, 179–180
Mindless person, 170
Morse code, 42

Noisy messages, 177

Perception(s)
    conscious and unconscious,
        126–127
    encoded, 187–188
Personal meaning, 24
Pet names, 41–42
Preconscious thoughts, 37–38
Prediction, 103–104
Primal scene, 74
Primary process, 32
    mechanisms of, 34–37
Projective identification, 177
Pseudo-insights, 163
Psychoanalytic cliché, 116

Quiet communication, 151
Quiet messages, 177

Receiver, 9
Reflection
  achieving insight through,
    188–190
  importance of, 187–188
Representability, 35, 49, 58
Repression, 38
  and dream formation, 66
Reverie, 180
Role evocation, 183–185

Scientific method, 27–28
Secondary process, 32
Secondary revision, 35, 58
Self-analysis, 196
  dumping inimical to, 191–192
  Freud's, 62–64
  procedures for, 191
Sender, 9
Slang, 42–43
Somatic expression, 125
Superego, 93
Survival, communication and,
    10
Symbiosis, healthy, 159
Symbolization, 34–35, 58, 60

Tape recording, 134–135,
    137–141
Technical meaning, 24
Thinking
  dynamically unconscious, 38
  magical, 92
  preconscious, 37–38
  primary-process, see Primary
    process
  secondary-process, see
    Secondary process
Transference, 89
Transversal communication, 105
Trigger(s), 72, 76–77
  and context, 50–51

emotional, 8
for fantasies, 38
hidden, 129–143
identification and analysis of,
    98–101
search for, 119–126
tape recording as, 137–141
Trigger decoding, 6, 95–102
balance between surface
    messages and, 107–108
of dreams, 119–127
validation of, 102–107
Truth(s)
  as functional lie, 115
  painful, 153–154
  search for, 158–160
  verification of, 25–28
Truth dumpers, 178, 181–182
Truth obliterator, 173–175,
    193–194
Truth receiver, 149, 153–160, 193
Truth sender, 148–149, 153–160,
    193–194

Unconscious encoding, 32–34
  in daily life, 69–78
  in a dream, 36–37
  indications of the presence of,
    79–88
  introduction to, 55–60
  origins with Freud, 61–67
  signs of, 70–71
Unconscious thoughts, 38

Validation, 27
  consensual, 28–29
  encoded, 142
  need for, 81
  via scientific method, 27–28
  in social settings, 102–107
  subjective factor in, 30
  by supporting evidence, 29–30